VOLUME EIGHT

Resting in the Heart
of the Savior

Direction for Our Times
As given to Anne,
a lay apostle

VOLUME EIGHT

Direction for Our Times
As given to Anne, a lay apostle

ISBN: 978-0-9766841-7-6

Library of Congress Number: Applied For

Publisher: Direction for Our Times

In Ireland:	In the USA:
Direction for Our Times	Direction for Our Times
The Hague Building	9000 West 81st Street
Cullies	Justice, IL 60458
Cavan	USA
Co. Cavan	
Ireland	
+353-(0)49-437-3040	708-496-9300

www.directionforourtimes.org

How to Pray the Rosary information, is used with permission. Copyright © Congregation of Marians of the Immaculate Conception, Stockbridge, MA 01263. www.marian.org.

Copy of the painting of *Madonna del Miracolo* reproduced with permission from the Church of Sant' Andrea delle Fratte, Rome.

Painting of *Jesus Christ the Returning King* by Janusz Antosz

V0713

Direction for Our Times wishes to manifest its complete obedience and submission of mind and heart to the final and definitive judgment of the Magisterium of the Catholic Church and the local Ordinary regarding the supernatural character of the messages received by Anne, a lay apostle.

In this spirit, the messages of Anne, a lay apostle, have been submitted to her bishop, Most Reverend Leo O'Reilly, Bishop of Kilmore, Ireland, and to the Vatican Congregation for the Doctrine of the Faith for formal examination. In the meantime Bishop O'Reilly has given permission for their publication.

DIOCESE OF KILMORE

Tel: 049 4331496
Fax: 049 4361796
Email: bishop@kilmorediocese.ie
Website: www.kilmorediocese.ie

Bishop's House
Cullies
Cavan
Co. Cavan

To Whom It May Concern:

Direction For Our Times (DFOT) is a religious movement founded by "Anne", a lay apostle from our diocese, who wishes to remain anonymous. The movement is in its infancy and does not as yet enjoy canonical status. I have asked a priest of the diocese, Fr.Connolly, to assist in the work of the movement and to ensure that in all its works and publications it remains firmly within the teaching and practice of the Catholic Church.

I have known "Anne", the founder of the movement, for several years. She is a Catholic in good standing in the diocese, a wife and mother of small children, and a woman of deep spirituality. From the beginning she has always been anxious that everything connected with the movement be subject to the authority of the Church. She has submitted all her writings to me and will not publish anything without my permission. She has submitted her writings to the Congregation of the Doctrine of the Faith and I have done so as well.

In so far as I am able to judge she is orthodox in her writings and teachings. Her spirituality and the spiritual path that she proposes to those who wish to accept it are in conformity with the teachings of the Church and of the great spiritual writers of the past and present.

Leo O'Reilly.

Date _16 June '06_

+Leo O'Reilly
Bishop of Kilmore

Diocesan Seal

DIOCESE OF KILMORE

Tel: 049-4331496
Fax: 049-4361796
Email: bishop@kilmorediocese.ie
Website: www.kilmorediocese.ie

Bishop's House
Cullies
Cavan
Co. Cavan

2 September 2011

To Whom It May Concern:

I offer an update on the present status of Anne, a lay apostle and Direction for Our Times.

I initially granted permission for the distribution of the messages and written materials of Anne. This position remains unchanged. The writings and materials may continue to be distributed. As pointed out in my letter on the DFOT website, the permission to distribute the messages does not imply a final judgment on whether they are authentic private revelation. A final judgment on that question must await the outcome of an official Church inquiry into these matters.

Following Church protocol, I set up a diocesan commission over a year ago to inquire into the writings of Anne and to evaluate her reports of receiving messages from heaven. That work of evaluation is continuing and the outcome of it will be made public in due course.

I hope this statement is helpful in the clarification of these matters.

Yours sincerely in Christ,

Leo O'Reilly
Bishop of Kilmore.

October 11, 2004

Dear Friends,

I am very much impressed with the messages delivered by Anne who states that they are received from God the Father, Jesus, and the Blessed Mother. They provide material for excellent and substantial meditation for those to whom they are intended, namely to the laity, to bishops and priests; and sinners with particular difficulties. These messages should not be read hurriedly but reserved for a time when heartfelt recollection and examination can be made.

I am impressed by the complete dedication of Anne to the authority of the magisterium, to her local Bishop and especially to the Holy Father. She is a very loyal daughter of the Church.

Sincerely in Christ,

Philip M. Hannan

Archbishop Philip M. Hannan, (Ret.)
President of FOCUS Worldwide Network
Retired Archbishop of New Orleans

PMH/sac

106 Metairie Lawn Dr. ● Metairie, LA 70001 ● Phone(504) 840-9898 ● Fax(504) 840-9818

Dr. Mark I. Miravalle, S.T.D.

Professor of Theology and Mariology, Franciscan University of Steubenville
313 High Street • Hopedale, OH 43976 • U.S.A.
740-937-2277 • mmiravalle@franciscan.edu

Without in any way seeking to anticipate the final and definitive judgment of the local bishop and of the Holy See (to which we owe our filial obedience of mind and heart), I wish to manifest my personal discernment concerning the nature of the messages received by "Anne," a Lay Apostle.

After an examination of the reported messages and an interview with the visionary herself, I personally believe that the messages received by "Anne" are of supernatural origin.

The message contents are in conformity with the faith and morals teachings of the Catholic Church's Magisterium and in no way violate orthodox Catholic doctrine. The phenomena of the precise manner of how the messages are transmitted (i.e., the locutions and visions) are consistent with the Church's historical precedence for authentic private revelation. The spiritual fruits (cf. Mt. 7:17-20) of Christian faith, conversion, love, and interior peace, based particularly upon a renewed awareness of the indwelling Christ and prayer before the Blessed Sacrament, have been significantly manifested in various parts of the world within a relatively brief time since the messages have been received and promulgated. Hence the principal criteria used by ecclesiastical commissions to investigate reported supernatural events (message, phenomena, and spiritual fruits) are, in my opinion, substantially satisfied in the case of "Anne's" experience.

The messages which speak of the coming of Jesus Christ, the "Returning King" do not refer to an imminent end of the world with Christ's final physical coming, but rather call for a spiritual receptivity to an ongoing spiritual return of Jesus Christ, a dynamic advent of Jesus which ushers in a time of extraordinary grace and peace for humanity (in ways similar to the Fatima promise for an eventual era of peace as a result of the Triumph of the Immaculate Heart of Mary, or perhaps the "new springtime" for the Church referred to by the words of the great John Paul II).

As "Anne" has received permission from her local ordinary, Bishop Leo O'Reilly, for the spreading of her messages, and has also submitted all her writings to the Congregation for the Doctrine of the Faith, I would personally encourage, (as the Church herself permits), the prayerful reading of these messages, as they have constituted an authentic spiritual benefit for a significant number of Catholic leaders throughout the world.

Mark I. Miravalle

Dr. Mark Miravalle
Professor of Theology and Mariology
Franciscan University of Steubenville
October 13, 2006

Table of Contents

Introduction

Dear Reader,

I am a wife, mother of six, and a Secular Franciscan.

At the age of twenty, I was divorced for serious reasons and with pastoral support in this decision. In my mid-twenties I was a single parent, working and bringing up a daughter. As a daily Mass communicant, I saw my faith as sustaining and had begun a journey toward unity with Jesus, through the Secular Franciscan Order or Third Order.

My sister travelled to Medjugorje and came home on fire with the Holy Spirit. After hearing of her beautiful pilgrimage, I experienced an even more profound conversion. During the following year I experienced various levels of deepened prayer, including a dream of the Blessed Mother, where she asked me if I would work for Christ. During the dream she showed me that this special spiritual work would mean I would be separated from others in the world. She actually showed me my extended family and how I would be separated from them. I told her that I did not care. I would do anything asked of me.

Shortly after, I became sick with endometriosis. I have been sick ever since, with one thing or another. My sicknesses are always the types that mystify doctors in the beginning. This is part of the cross and I mention it because so many suffer in this way. I was told by my doctor that I would never conceive children. As a single parent, this did not concern me as I assumed it was God's will. Soon after, I met a wonderful man. My first marriage had been annulled and we married and conceived five children.

Spiritually speaking, I had many experiences that included what I now know to be interior locutions. These moments were beautiful and the words still stand out firmly in my heart, but I did not get excited because I was busy offering up illnesses and exhaustion. I took it as a matter of course that Jesus had to work hard to sustain me as He had given me a lot to handle. In looking back, I see that He was preparing me to do His work. My preparation period was long, difficult and not very exciting. From the outside, I think people thought, man, that woman has bad luck. From the inside, I saw that while my sufferings were painful and long lasting, my little family was growing in love, in size and in wisdom, in the sense that my husband and I certainly understood what was important and what was not important. Our continued crosses did that for us.

Various circumstances compelled my husband and me to move with our children far from my loved ones. I offered this up and must say it is the most difficult thing I have had to contend with. Living in exile brings many beautiful opportunities to align with Christ's will; however, you have to continually remind yourself that you are doing that. Otherwise you just feel sad. After several years in exile, I finally got the inspiration to go to Medjugorje. It was actually a gift from my husband for my fortieth birthday. I had tried to go once before, but circumstances prevented the trip and I understood it was not God's will. Finally, though, it was time and my eldest daughter and I found ourselves in front of St. James Church. It was her second trip to Medjugorje.

I did not expect or consider that I would experience anything out of the ordinary. At any rate, we had a beautiful five days. I experienced a spiritual healing on the mountain. My daughter rested and prayed. A quiet but significant thing happened to me. During my Communions, I spoke with Jesus conversationally. I thought this was beautiful, but it had happened before on occasion so I was not stunned or overcome. I remember telling others that Communions in Medjugorje were powerful. I came home, deeply grateful to Our Lady for bringing us there.

The conversations continued all that winter. At some time in the six months that followed our trip, the conversations leaked into my life and came at odd times throughout the day. Jesus began to direct me with decision and I found it more and more difficult to refuse when He asked me to do this or that. I told no one.

During this time, I also began to experience direction from the Blessed Mother. Their voices are not hard to distinguish. I do not hear them in an auditory way, but in my soul or mind. By this time I knew that something remarkable was occurring and Jesus was telling me that He had special work for me, over and above my primary vocation as wife and mother. He told me to write the messages down and that He would arrange to have them published and disseminated. Looking back, it took Him a long time to get me comfortable enough where I was willing to trust Him. I trust His voice now and will continue to do my best to serve Him, given my constant struggle with weaknesses, faults, and the pull of the world.

Please pray for me as I continue to try to serve Jesus. Please answer "yes" to Him because He so badly needs us and He is so kind. He will take you right into His heart if you let Him. I am praying for you and am so grateful to God that He has given you these words. Anyone who knows Him must fall in love with Him, such is His goodness. If you have been struggling, this is your answer. He is coming to you in a special way through these words and the graces that flow through them.

Please do not fall into the trap of thinking that He cannot possibly mean for you to reach high levels of holiness. As I say somewhere in my writings, the greatest sign of the times is Jesus having to make do with the likes of me as His secretary. I consider myself the B-team, dear friends. Join me and together we will do our little bit for Him.

Message received from Jesus immediately following my writing of the above biographical information:

You see, My child, that you and I have been together for a long time. I was working quietly in your life for years before you began this work. Anne, how I love you. You can look back through your life and see so many "yes" answers to Me. Does that not please you and make you glad? You began to say "yes" to Me long before you experienced extraordinary graces. If you had not, My dearest, I could never have given you the graces or assigned this mission to you. Do you see how important it was that you got up every day, in your ordinary life, and said "yes" to your God, despite difficulty, temptation, and hardship? You could not see the big plan as I saw it. You had to rely on your faith. Anne, I tell you today, it is still that way. You cannot see My plan, which is bigger than your human mind can accept. Please continue to rely on your faith as it brings Me such glory. Look at how much I have been able to do with you, simply because you made a quiet and humble decision for Me. Make another quiet and humble decision on this day and every day, saying, "I will serve God." Last night you served Me by bringing comfort to a soul in pain. You decided against yourself and for Me, through your service to him. There was gladness in heaven, Anne. You are Mine. I am yours. Stay with Me, My child. Stay with Me.

The Allegiance Prayer
For All Lay Apostles

Dear God in heaven, I pledge my allegiance to You. I give You my life, my work and my heart. In turn, give me the grace of obeying Your every direction to the fullest possible extent. Amen.

On the Nature of Private Revelation

When reading these messages it is always important to understand them within the context of the Church's teaching on revelation as a whole. We gain some insight into how to understand private revelation from a theological commentary on the message of Fatima written by Pope Benedict XVI when he was Prefect of the Congregation for the Doctrine of the Faith.

"Message of Fatima" provides us with valuable direction into the process of understanding private revelation and its purpose. He rightly anticipates the questions that emerge for us in its contemplation and offers guidance in the task of prudent interpretation.

What is the difference between Public and private Revelation?

Cardinal Ratzinger begins by distinguishing public Revelation from private revelation and their theological status. Public Revelation in the form of the Old and New Testament is complete. *"In Christ God has said everything, that is, he has revealed himself completely, and therefore, Revelation came to an end with the fulfillment of the mystery of Christ as enunciated in the New Testament."* Revelation, God's revealing himself to man, is complete and given to us in the Gospels.

Nevertheless, he points out, referring to the Catechism of the Catholic Church that, *"...even if Revelation is complete, it has not been made fully explicit. It remains for Christian faith to gradually grasp its full significance over the course of centuries (66)"*. In this context we can understand the role of private revelation. It is part of the process of grasping, which assists in the gradual understanding, of Public Revelation. In short, it assists us in a given period of history to understand what God has already revealed to us in Christ and in how to live the Gospel during this time.

How should we respond to Revelation?

Pope Benedict speaks about how we, as followers of Christ, should respond to revelation. Public Revelation requires the assent of Catholic faith, divine faith, because in it God speaks his word to us in human words. *"Faith in God and in his word is different to any other human faith, trust or opinion."*

In relation to approved private revelations, he goes on to say, quoting Cardinal Lambertini, later Pope Benedict XIV, *"An assent of Catholic Faith is not due to revelations approved in this way; it is not even possible. These revelations seek rather an assent of human faith in keeping with the requirements of prudence, which puts them before us as probable and credible to piety."* Regarding the role of such private revelations, he says: *"Such a message can be a genuine help in understanding the Gospel and living it better at a particular moment in time; therefore it should not be disregarded. It is a help which is offered, but which one is not obliged to use."*

How should we understand prophecy?

As well as understanding its relationship to public Revelation, the nature of private revelation itself is of significance in helping us towards its prudent interpretation. Private revelation can contain elements to be understood literally or symbolically, and also both. Cardinal Ratzinger quotes Cardinal Sodano concerning visions, *"[they] do not describe photographically events in the future, but synthesize and compress against a single background facts which extend through time in an unspecified succession and duration."* Here he is articulating for us that the images and visions contained in private revelation have layers of meaning that are not necessarily bound in time and space in our human sense of them. Cardinal Ratzinger further states, *"not every element of the vision has to have a historical sense. It is the vision as a whole that matters...the center is found where the vision becomes a summons and guide to the will of God."* From this we can gain insight into both the nature of the images and their capacity to be symbolic and multifaceted, but also and more importantly, the purpose of them-*"...a summons and guide to the will of God"* and *"to help us to understand the signs of the times and to respond to them rightly in faith."* Further to this he states, *"Prediction of the future is of secondary importance...what is of primary importance is the declaration of God's will for the present time."*

In a recent address concerning the figurative language used by Jesus in St. Mark's Gospel, chapter 13, Pope Benedict XVI states:

"For this reason Jesus does not describe the end of the world and when he uses apocalyptic images he does not conduct himself like a "visionary." On the contrary, he wants to take away the curiosity of his disciples in every age about dates and predictions and wishes instead to give them a key to a deep, essential reading, and above all to indicate the right path to take, today and tomorrow, to enter into eternal life."

Our understandable 'curiosity' should not become a distraction from the deeply personal and meaningful contact which awaits us in the Gospels and which private revelation ushers us toward ...*"what is essential is the actualization of definitive Revelation, which concerns me at the deepest level."*

Sections of this Volume refer to the darkness which will encircle the earth and speak in terms similar to many places in Sacred Scripture using a genre of writing known as apocalyptic. It is helpful therefore to understand these writings within the context of Revelation contained in Sacred Scripture. We encourage you to read the following passages as you read this book. They are as follows: Mark 13:24-27, 32, Matthew 24:29-31, 36, Luke 21:25-28, 29-33, 2 Peter 3:10 and frequently throughout the book of Revelation.

In summary:

- God revealed Himself in divine Revelation. This Revelation is found in the Scriptures and the Tradition of the Church.

- The response that divine Revelation requires of Christians is the assent of Catholic faith, i.e. divine faith.

- Divine Revelation, which took place in Christ, is complete but it has not been made fully explicit.

- Private revelation does not add anything new to the deposit of faith. It has a role in making divine Revelation explicit. It also assists us in a given period of history in understanding what God has already revealed to us in Christ and in how to live the gospel during this time.

- Private revelations seek an assent of human

faith in keeping with the requirements of prudence, which puts them before us as probable and credible to piety.

- Private revelation is a help which is offered but which one is not obliged to use.

- Private revelation can contain elements to be understood literally or symbolically.

- In regard to visions, prediction of the future is of secondary importance. What is of primary importance is the declaration of God's will for the present time.

Anne's Introduction to Volume 8

In the following Volume we are blessed to get a glimpse into the way in which Jesus views many situations in our world. This blessing carries with it a responsibility to alter our actions where necessary. This is always the way in life. There is a constant call for conversion and advancement in holiness.

When the Lord shows me a vision, I see the smallest part of a big situation. In the heaven visions, for example, I would think I had seen it all and that there could not possibly be anything left that I had not experienced or that I needed to experience. Then the Lord would show me something else that opened up a whole new area of thought and divine knowledge.

I often think of someone being given a leaf to study. We could spend years studying this leaf because it is such a miracle of creation, given its unique color, function, structure, chemical make-up, and relationship to the plant on which it grows. Despite this, we cannot say based solely on the study of one leaf that we understand a forest. The study of this leaf gives us clues to the forest and to the nature of the forest, of course, and we take these clues and rejoice in the understanding that some day perhaps we will study and understand the forest in its entirety.

I believe these visions are similar. They are intended to give us insight into the heart of Jesus. He is very much present in each day. He is present in our world. We believe this and it is true. Brothers and sisters, we must spend time considering the ramifications of this fact. Jesus is not present as a stone, cold and unfeeling, but as our God, filled with love and compassion for us. Just as Jesus is filled with love and compassion for each one of us, He is filled with love and compassion for all of those around us, including those we hurt, those we reject, those we judge and those we fail to love. Jesus is woundable in His body, meaning in you and me. If we are wounded, it hurts Jesus. He feels pain with us and for us. He also feels terribly the pain of rejection when we turn our back to Him.

It is of this that the Lord seeks to remind us. He is paying attention. We must try not to wound Him. Those of us called, and that includes everyone reading these words, must try to comfort Him by bringing others back to His heart.

How do we do that? Do we approach others and tell them that they are getting it wrong and that we have it right? That if they become like us then, and only then, they will be acceptable to Christ? No, my friends. We know better than that.

We work first in our own soul, and through that work and because of that work the Lord is able to flow through us into the world. If we concentrate on becoming holy and spending time in silence with Christ, there is a better chance that we are working on His agenda and not our own. We must look constantly to our vocations. Every day there must be some time spent considering if we are being faithful to our vocations as mothers, fathers, priests, religious, single apostles. Who has the Lord placed to walk with us? Who are the people in our lives we are called to love each day? Where are we failing? Where can we improve? If we do this work with Christ, He will make us saints and we will take our part in the Renewal.

A few words about the mystical experience of visions and locutions.

Visions

I experience these visions at the Lord's call. I cannot will these experiences and I do not ask for them. The Lord tells me that He wishes to bring me somewhere or show me something. I see the vision in my soul, in other words, not with my eyes. The Lord remains with me throughout, explaining what I am seeing or answering my questions. The Lord will often direct me to note particular details. I have recorded them to the best of my ability and with consideration as to what I feel is the Lord's point in showing me the vision. I know that the Lord wills these experiences not simply for my benefit, but for the benefit of us all.

I add that I do not experience these things separately from the Lord. I am acutely aware, in each vision, of how the Lord is viewing the scene and feeling about it. If the Lord feels pain at the situation, I am allowed to feel His pain. If the Lord feels joy, I am allowed to feel His joy.

The experiences and locutions recorded in Volume Eight occurred over a period of time. The Lord then gave locutions for the beginning and end of the Volume and gave me instruction as to their placement.

Locutions

I experience a locution as a conversation or communication in my soul. I do not hear the words with my ears. The experience of a locution is as distinct from an inspiration as talking is distinct from listening. If God is talking, I am listening. If Our Lady is talking, I am listening. If I am responding, God is listening or Our Lady is listening. There is no confusion. I know who is speaking.

Infusions

In addition to the times when heaven communicates through locutions, there are times when heaven communicates by placing concepts or knowledge in my soul in order to give me an immediate understanding or enlightenment. The experience of any heavenly communication is accompanied by, and is in itself, a vast grace that imprints itself upon the soul and creates a peace, along with a willingness to serve. After a heavenly communication or locution I feel calm and trusting, with a sense of purpose about what the Lord has communicated.

As I understand my role in this process, I am to report back to those who are open to hearing and accepting.

Apostles should ask the Holy Spirit to be with them as they consider these writings.

Chastisements

With regard to chastisements, I think we must concentrate on the fact that one way or another we will all die. When we die, we will lose everything from an earthly standpoint. We will not be carrying suitcases to heaven. This is our time on earth so it must be the perfect time for each of us to be here. When it is the perfect time for us to be finished on earth, Jesus will come for us.

Jesus gives us advance warning of changes to help us to begin a process of detachment from material things. He also intends to help us to accept any difficulties in accordance with His view and His goals. We must learn to look at every situation in the world through the eyes of Jesus and become more accustomed to seeing things from the heavenly viewpoint. In this way, we will gain the benefits the Lord intends for us and also assist others in using all experiences to progress in holiness. Jesus is giving us advance instruction on how to conduct ourselves.

In particular, the Lord is looking to train lay apostles to respond to every event in their lives with His calm acceptance so that we can spread that calm acceptance throughout the world.

I pray that people will accept God's words in whatever way God is speaking to them. I know that the Renewal in the world is gaining strength and momentum. I know it will continue to gain strength and momentum. I pray that all apostles will answer God's call to the fullest possible extent.

September 20, 2004
Jesus

My dear children, I will not leave you in darkness. I seek to bring you to the Light. In order to do so, I pull you in, close against My heart. Do you want to be with Me? I am suffering in this time, so those who are close to Me will also suffer. Far better, My friends, to suffer the pangs of the Savior, than to wander in darkness. Come rest in My heart so that I may show you My pain.

September 13, 2004
Jesus

My heart suffers because of the darkness of your world. Souls distance themselves from Me until they no longer feel the pangs of longing. Goodness has been driven from their hearts by too long spent in the coldness of this earthly spiritual vacuum. You are dead to Me, dear souls, and I cannot bear it. Come back to Jesus. I am He. I am Jesus and My heart feels the anguish of your rejection. I want you to be healed. I want to give you an opportunity to feel My presence again so that you can make a choice based on Truth. If you feel My presence in your soul and you then reject Me, so be it. I will accept your decision. But you must decide that for yourself and not be tricked. You see, My enemy has deluded you. He has fooled you. The enemy of goodness, the prince of all that is dark, seeks to snatch My beloved ones. I will not allow this. I am giving the greatest push right now to take you back to My heart. You will find complete love and forgiveness. In My heart is every explanation you require to understand that you belong in heaven with your family. Because it is time to return to Me, My dearest one, I send you a bundle of graces. You are being given every possible opportunity to look at Me and know that I am your Savior. I love you so much that I am in pain at this separation. I want your love so badly. Please. Look up to Me and seek Me. Ask Me to reveal Myself. Ask Me to show Myself to you. I am here, waiting.

September 14, 2004

Today I saw a woman in prayer. She was kneeling in a Eucharistic Adoration chapel, in rapt consideration of the Eucharist. Her face was peaceful. This woman had suffered a great deal from a lifetime of separation from Jesus. Because of the messages and graces, she has been brought back to Jesus' heart. I felt such joy looking at her. Jesus showed me that the woman was someone for whom I had prayed. She had suffered terribly. This is a vision of the future. Jesus is showing me what is going to happen in her life. I am grateful.

Jesus

I know you are grateful. I show this to the world because I want the world to have hope. Yes, I am suffering. Yes, many souls are in darkness but this is an example of how a soul can be rescued. How many souls are there like her? That is up to you, My little apostles. You must seek out those who are wounded and give them My words. These words are heavenly balm for the wounds that this current darkness has inflicted on My beloved children. I am showing you My heart so it is only fair that I show you the joy in My heart when I consider the return and the healing of a soul who has suffered. Share in My joy. Rejoice in her return, for she was lost and now she is found.

To those of you who still ache from separation from Me, I say, "Return." You see that My heart experiences joy. I am joyful now and I will be joyful again when I see you at peace, with your face transfused by heavenly contemplation. This is a time of labor, a time of service. Keep your course set on the heavenly mission at all times and together We will fill My churches with beautiful souls such as this one. Rejoice, My friends. Rejoice.

I am delighted at such a happy day in the heart of Jesus. It has just occurred to me that it is the feast of the Triumph of the Cross.

September 15, 2004
Jesus

Today, especially, we celebrate and venerate Our Mother as Our Lady of Sorrows. Dear children, just as I suffer at the distance many souls have placed between themselves and heaven, our Mother also suffers. She, more than anyone, shared My Passion. She now shares My anguish at the loss of so many souls. I feel revulsion at the sins of this world. Our Mother shares this revulsion. You must understand that when you are glimpsing My heart, and My feelings, you are also glimpsing the Immaculate Heart of Mary. This precious and pure little heart beats with love and tenderness for each of us. Every soul is precious to Mary.

I thank you for all of the little sacrifices that console Me. I want you to know that each prayer and sacrifice given for Me also consoles our Mother. Great joy comes to Mary when souls give thanks and praise to Me. Truly, if you are devoted to My Mother, and I want you to be, work for Me and she will be happy with you. She seeks only My will and her active and powerful intercession in your world furthers My will in a spectacular fashion. She is the woman clothed with the sun, capable of vanquishing the enemy.

September 16, 2004

Today I saw a young soldier. He was hiding in a small place, obviously frightened. There was a battle going on around him and he was resting, panting and sweating. He was not anxious or panicked, but you could tell that he was in a difficult situation and he well knew it. He began to organize himself to make a move.

Jesus

He is to hand over his life today. You see that he is frightened. In his humanity he fears physical pain and suffering. This is natural. This young man is aware in his soul that he will join Me on this day. He knows Me well, you see, and I have been whispering to him for some time. He is prepared. While he is fearful in his humanity, his soul is at peace.

This boy has walked with Me throughout his life. He did not avoid sin each day, but he knew sin for sin and always made peace with Me. He has been given spiritual formation by parents who respected Me and understood their duty to pass on their faith to their son. As a result, their son faces his death with quiet acceptance. He will shortly know joy. He is not distressed, as you see, despite his knowledge that his time on earth is over. He is comfortable that he has done his best. Anne, I tell you, this young man is beautiful to Me. In your world he would not be known as exceptional in any way. In the heavenly Kingdom he will be a saint. His parents will grieve his loss, but I will console them and they, in turn, will know peace and joy in their souls. They have done well by their son and he gives them great glory. Was his life too short? How could it be, when I, Myself, ordained the duration of his time on earth? He served Me in the time he was allotted and all is right with him. I tell you with the greatest seriousness that this young man is far more blessed than some of his peers who will survive this day. His soul is safe.

September 17, 2004

Today our Lord showed me a classroom filled with small children. They were very beautiful, as small children are, and I felt our Lord's powerful and total love for each one of them. He showed me how He suffers because He is being denied access to them.

Jesus

They are not told about Me, Anne. They are filled instead with worldly notions that change from week to week, as worldly souls argue and compete for the honor of creating an ideology. They, the people who create these thoughts leading nowhere, are puffed up with pride. The schools of nonsense manufactured by worldly souls soothe their consciences and feed their sinfulness. Children are often far more discerning than adults and My little ones are confused at worst. At best they learn nothing. My pain at this is severe and touches the core of My Sacred Heart.

You saw how I worked so powerfully in the soul of the soldier who spent his life making his way to Me. I cannot do that in these small children. They will wander aimlessly through their lives. Certainly, in My mercy, I will secure access to them at some time, but I want more than that for them. I want more than that for each one of you. Bring Me to the children, dear servants of heaven. Bring Me to the smallest members of God's Kingdom so that I may take My rightful place in their souls. You see the fruits of My absence in their lives. Your youth are not happy. They are in anguish at the separation from their God. I am also in anguish at this separation. I suffer for their pain and confusion. Dear servants, these poor souls do not even know the source of their pain. They know simply that something they require has not been given to them. I am that Something. You will not fix these children with worldly notions. They need Me.

May 25, 2004

Our God is prepared to act in order to cleanse the world. He would be justified in destroying the world, such is the level of rebellion against Him. Because of His great love for us, He cannot bear to do that, but He is allowing change and the angels prepare to act. Jesus says that in times past, even as near as the first half of the twentieth century, souls were generally obedient. This is not so anymore. During this time, souls are generally disobedient.

May 26, 2004

Jesus showed me His deep disappointment at the sight of many of today's mothers. He gave me a glimpse of the heart of a mother who was heedless to the needs of her children and overly concerned with things of this world and of her appearance, as in physical appearance. This was disturbing. Jesus told me that this mother, who is representative of many, lacks love for her children and loves herself. He indicated her heart, which was like a cracked stone with small serpents moving through the cracks. I hate serpents and this vision was very unpleasant. The serpents represented pride, avarice, jealousy or envy, hatred, etc. Jesus was greatly disappointed as He showed me the children who are emotionally abandoned and receiving indifference when they are in need of and entitled to warmth and love. I felt revulsion at the sight of this woman, but again, she was representative of many modern women. I must say that on the outside this woman was quite beautiful.

While this woman was repulsing me, Jesus moved on to show His opinion or experience of many modern men. He said they ignore their own spiritual duties and often completely abandon any formation of their children. He indicated great sins of the sexual nature, some with complicit partners, but also many assaults on innocent victims.

Jesus told me He is with every innocent victim, always. He said He hears every cry and each act will have to be atoned for. Jesus is disgusted and repulsed by these sins, but does not turn His face away, because He must witness every act on earth.

Jesus then said, *"Because you are My apostle, you are entitled to joy, so I will now give you joy and show you what gives Me joy."*

Jesus showed me the heart of a woman apostle. It had no open cracks in it and was like beautiful warm marble. This heart was well protected by its owner through prayer and service and Jesus felt joy and happiness upon the contemplation of this soul. This was a modern apostle who was attempting to follow Him. I could see that there had been cracks in the past but they were well sealed and closed by prayers and sacrifices and acts of unselfishness. They were healed. These cracks, where sin had formerly left openings, did not bother Jesus in the least. On the contrary, they were signs of how the soul had turned away from sin and had followed Him.

Jesus then showed me that while He was surveying the sins of both men and women today, and filled with just anger, there was a constant tugging at His sleeve. This distracting tugging came from the prayers of souls in Eucharistic Adoration. These prayers distracted Him from His just anger and deflected great calamities from befalling this world.* Chastisements have been mitigated in this

---

* Both the Old and New Testaments reflect the idea that natural disasters and calamities may at times be God's way of allowing man to experience consequences from sin which can act as purification and ultimately lead people back to Him. We have always been taught through Scripture and Tradition that God can avert much suffering through the prayers of the faithful.

way. He showed me Our Lady, who was collecting poor wounded souls from this world of darkness. She was drying tears, healing wounds, and then instructing souls on what they could do to best serve Jesus and help them to save others. This was so beautiful and did make me happy and joyful, despite the ugliness of the first parts.

Jesus told me that in Eucharistic Adoration, His graces flow into souls, who then go back into the world, where His graces then flow into their homes, work places, and peer groups. He said that in the most difficult cases, where an adorer is still sinful, He can preserve their families and limit the damage this person does to others while also healing and preserving the person. In the best cases, where the person accepts His grace and lives a pious life, He can truly change areas of the world.

He showed me that the more souls we have in Eucharistic Adoration, the more the river of purity will cleanse the world.

May 27, 2004

Jesus showed me the world, with layers of sin, like layers of smog that lay above us. He explained to me that as a holy personage, He actually experienced a stench near sin and sinful behaviors. He said that the holier one became, the more apparent this experience was and that holy souls on earth also felt this, but only souls who have reached a very high level of holiness. Where there was holiness, the smog was pierced, and shafts of light from heaven came through. The greater the holiness, the greater the light. He said that enormous light and graces flowed down into the words of the Volumes and that as these words were spread, we would see more and more and more shafts of light piercing the ugly smog of sin. I said, "Great. So maybe there is no need for any other cleansing." But no, this grace is so souls will be prepared for the cleansing.

Jesus' heart is very heavy and I felt badly because it was difficult for me to get away and I was a little resentful at having to go down to do this work. I apologized. He said, ***"Do not deny the Savior the small bit of comfort He gains from your companionship."*** Poor Jesus. I will try in the future not to be so distracted.

He indicated the red glowing moon and I felt dread. He said there would come a great stillness in the souls of the just. The foolish will make jokes. At that time, every just soul will hear the voice of the Savior as I do if He needs to instruct them. He said we, the just, would prepare to hand our lives to Him. This is wisdom from the Spirit. He said Our Lady will be before the Throne of God pleading for graces like a mother who seeks to bring her children to safety before a great storm. He said she has terrific power before this Throne. Jesus is so sad. He does not want this but will not prevent it any longer. I begged Him to tell me how to comfort Him. He said, *"You comfort Me with cheerful obedience."*

May 30, 2004*
Jesus

Immediately following the darkness comes a day of the greatest freshness. All of nature will be renewed and will bear the signs of God's presence. This will be a stark contrast to the debris left by the forces of evil. People remaining, holy people, will have a difficult time in the immediate period because they will have adjustments to make. The same conveniences and comforts will not be available and daily tasks will change. This is not important, though, because people will be connected to God in the most beautiful fashion. This will bring great joy and peace, and will compensate people for the great changes they have had to witness. Remember that many souls will have been taken by events prior to this time, so the population will be smaller than in your world today, as of this writing. If I desire that a child be protected, that child will be placed with holy souls.

*In understanding the entries May 30, 2004, June 1, 2004 and June 2, 2004 it may be helpful for the reader to read the Book of Revelation chapter 20.

21

June 1, 2004

After the time of darkness, there will come a very difficult time for the remaining people. There will be great diseases, despite God's guidance, and another group of people again will be taken. This is the final cleansing. The people remaining after this immediate period will be holy committed souls and they will begin the time of the Great Obedience. They will work hard for their survival but will do so in joy. Some advances will be kept from the period before the darkness, including advances in hygiene, with regard to water and sewage and medicine, but many of the conveniences we enjoy today will not be maintained, as in the speed with which modern man currently communicates. It will not be God's will that the post-darkness man be in constant communication with others because he will be in more constant communication with God and heaven. Man will not struggle with constant temptation to sin because of the media as it does today.

June 2, 2004

In the new time the world will be different. The world will be governed, generally, from Rome where the Holy Father will reside.* Jesus will be ruling through the Holy Father and will communicate in a more direct fashion. There will still be individual nations but not as many as there are today. People will be obedient to God and He will guide souls more directly. People will see this presence quite clearly in a way they do not at this time. For example, when they look on grass or a beautiful tree, they will think, "God is good," and "God is the Creator." Death will be viewed with great tranquility and peace, whereas now it is seen as the greatest of tragedies. Generally there will be obedience.

Jesus said that in the new time, if a person made a movie that was in any way impure, nobody would go to see it and that person would be scorned. There will be sin, but nothing, NOTHING, to compare to the sin in today's world.

Jesus said that one of the things that caused Him the most pain is that His mother is treated disrespectfully. In the new time she will be loved and honored and she will be very active with youth. This

*Note of explanation by Anne: If the Church in the new time gives a direction, a correction, or an instruction, the people, in this pure spirit of obedience, will follow in love and gratitude, correctly identifying the leaders in the Church as representatives of Jesus Christ. This spirit of obedience present in the Body of Christ, the people, will actually at times adjust the course of the world. This is what I mean when I write that the world will be governed, generally, from Rome.

will please Him of course. I asked Him how He would feel during this new time and He said, *"I will feel content."*

Because of the good will and obedience of the time, the saints will be able to be quite active in the lives of those on earth. It will be wonderful and Jesus said He is telling us this to give us hope.[†]

[†]Note of explanation by Anne: As I understand the future of the Church, it will be lifted up to its proper place of honor in our world. This will occur, not through any aggressive or authoritarian action or disposition of this Church. Quite the contrary. The Church will be lifted up through the love and fidelity and unity of Catholics, lay, clergy and religious. These people will mystically lift the Church. This does not mean there will be no sin or an absence of free will, but a general air of obedience, love and joy in our relationship with Christ. People will have a more connected relationship with Christ. They will be united to Him in prayer in a more pronounced fashion than they are now and will love the Church and live peacefully in the safety of its direction. This is obedience. God's people will recognize His dominion over us and our world. The Church will greatly impact the world in that Catholics will move in unity with Jesus Christ and the Church and not against it. There will be a general air of Christian unity.

June 4, 2004
Jesus

As My words flow through your fingers, so My graces will flow through your hands. The enemy speaks lies. My truth will burst through your lips in response. All is well. I take you into My soul and you are caught up in the fires of My Sacred Heart. When I return you to your own soul, you are more Me than you. So it will be because I have willed it.

June 9, 2004

In the immediate future we will see an even greater attack on purity. It will be directed at women and children as are all such attacks. The greatest attack on purity is seen in the sin of abortion. Jesus told me that the act of abortion is actually the devil's rage unleashed in the greatest fashion. The devil so hates God and all that is good and holy that he has actually persuaded mankind to destroy developing life. I sensed Jesus suffering terribly and asked Him if I could be with Him to at least keep Him company and that is when He told me this. He said abortion is the devil's greatest fury and a direct attack on God the Creator. Jesus suffered terribly for this sin during His Passion and said that abortion alone would be responsible for a terrible punishment on the world, one which He is allowing because of the sin of abortion. Jesus often steps in and prevents mankind from reaping the full price that is owed from sin, but in this case He will not mitigate. He said any work done to prevent or stop abortions would be greatly rewarded. He repeated that statement twice.

June 10, 2004

Jesus again spoke of abortion and how the sacred place of the womb belongs to God the Creator. He said that He has allowed many medical and scientific advances out of mercy and love for mankind, but some men, in cooperation with the enemy, who has secured their service through things like greed and pride, have exploited and desecrated these medical and scientific gifts. He said this is evident in that the enemy has pierced the sacredness of the womb to destroy the work of the Creator, and has attempted to become the creator by himself, in defiance to God, by creating members of humanity. Jesus said that the people responsible know that they are committing grave sin. He said He puts holy men and women in their paths to warn them, but some continue down this path of terrible disobedience. Jesus said that many men and women have desisted from these activities because their consciences have warned them that their behaviors were sinful. These people will receive great forgiveness and reward in heaven, particularly those who then repent and speak out against these actions.

Jesus then began to talk about how mankind is so arrogant that he thinks God cannot take all of these advances away. He can, of course, and He said that He intends to do just that, but only for a short time. He said that He is too merciful to permanently destroy our ability to assist earthly souls with the fields of medicine and science.

Jesus showed me that another thing causing Him great sadness today is loneliness in families. He said, *"Look. These children have no one to play with because the siblings I willed for them have been rejected by their parents. Selfish generation. They fear that additional children will impede their entertainment. The elderly are also a burden because, despite the fact that these same souls have limited their number of children, they still have not gained sufficient entertainment time so they must also leave the care of their elderly parents to others, even in situations where they could care for them themselves. Both their children and their parents experience loss in this situation. I feel only sadness at this."*

Jesus also said that time hung heavily on these souls because they are not involved in heavenly activities. He told me that no entertainment will be enough to satisfy these people. We must pray for them because they are chasing nothings. Jesus is pleased by selflessness and said that people should experience great entertainment in each other, meaning in their families and with their loved ones. This time with loved ones is not supposed to be such a burden as it is treated today.

Today Jesus talked to me about the darkness. He said that it would originate in hell and for that time, the duration of the darkness, the world would be entombed in this darkness from hell. It originates in hell but is allowed to flow out into the world for this period of time, encircling the world until it meets and the darkness is total. This darkness is black and is the total absence of light. I keep trying to stress the blackness but that is because it is so total and complete that I am not sure if people can really grasp its density or completeness. I do not understand this concept of total evil but Jesus assures me that some people will welcome this darkness and exult in it. He said some will know demons by name because they have affiliations with them already. I heard an example of the most horrid screams and screeches, like a wild cat would make. These demons will perform the vilest of tortures upon people. These are not the people of the Light, by the way. I am to see our experience of this time later. During this time, truly hell has come to earth. Jesus does not want this or will it, but He definitely is allowing this and it is a part of His justice. The evil souls in the world are resting upon the grace of God, despite their mockery of it. They are laughing at God but it is God who keeps them protected and comfortable on the earth while they practice all kinds of sin and deception. In other words, while they are living like demons, they are enjoying the fruits of God's goodness. This is so temporary and they will reap what they are sowing soon indeed. I am trying to think of a good analogy so that others can understand this.

You are eating the wonderful food from your host's

banquet, all the while making fun of and scorning your host, who continues to feed you. You abuse the host's children terribly, in full view of the host, while laughing at him and as it were DARING him to act. You are taking advantage of the host's good manners, as evil people so often do now. The host is about to act and the host's enemies are about to get thrown out of the gathering. They will then no longer be able to prey on God's good people who do not fight back in the same way because they follow Christ.

They will not be able to practice their evil in the same way when they are surrounded by people like themselves. This will happen during the time of darkness. If they call out to Jesus, He will answer them. The really prideful people will not call out to Jesus because they hate Jesus. I cannot even fathom who these people are or why they would choose hell over Christ but He assures me that this is exactly what is occurring. The saints will be gathered before the Throne during this time, as will all of heaven, begging God to end the darkness quickly. There will be satanic sacrifices and offerings all over the earth during this time of the most abominable evil.

June 10, 2004—Later

Jesus told me that during the time of darkness holy souls will be gathered together and that souls who barely know each other will be placed together per His instructions. He said that much has been written about this time of darkness in the past, but that He does not want to generate fear and that fear is neither necessary nor appropriate if you are following His path. He said that young children will sleep and that adults will pray constantly, but not from terror. Adults will be experiencing union with Jesus, hearing His voice, so they will find it easy and will desire to remain in constant prayer. Jesus said that you would not go outside during this time in the same way you would not go outside during a violent storm because it would not be safe. He also said though that holy souls should not worry about being attacked by demons because demons are repelled by prayer, holiness, and holy souls. Demons will not want to be near those places where there are holy souls gathered in prayer. Because hell will be emptied and kind of loosed on the earth, it will be a conflagration of evil on earth, and that this is the big mardi gras of evil if you will, where evil on earth will destroy itself.

After the abomination, committed by the man Jesus spoke to me about, Jesus will end the darkness, the earth will be cleansed, and the time of the Great Disobedience will be at an end, giving way to a time of peace and obedience on the earth, which will last for a long time. A great many events will transpire before this darkness, including the signs that Jesus has referred to.

June 14, 2004

Jesus allowed me to see that He is sad. He grows weary with this world and with the constant disregard for His presence in and dominion over this world. Where there was once general love, there is general hatred. Jesus again allowed me to glimpse the wrath He has for those who destroy innocence. Initially, He made reference to children who have been molested. His wrath at offenders in this area of sin is going to be fearsome. I do not know how to convey in words the gravity of this. He said they should REPENT. This is a most serious situation for these offenders. He said they would do better to do violence to themselves than to assault a child. He also said something else about this. He said that at this time He is releasing a torrent of graces for the healing of the souls of children and adults who have been molested in this way. As never before, He will grant peace to victims of this type of crime against innocence. Victims themselves can ask for these graces and those who know people who have been hurt in this way can secure these graces. Please ask Jesus for these graces because they are available.

June 18, 2004

Jesus told me that His Sacred Heart beats and can pump mercy into the world. I had an awareness of His heart beating. This costs Him effort. I suffered terribly and said, finally, "Jesus, what is it?"

He replied, *"It is indifference that causes you such anguish. The world does not accept My mercy, but walks away from it as if the shedding of My Precious Blood was just another meaningless trifle to be discarded. You suffer so severely because of the indifference of souls in your world this day. The suffering Savior thanks you."*

I asked Him if He would be consoled if others joined at this time to share in His suffering because I know there are many other people who would be willing to do this.

He said, *"No. I do not will this type of suffering for all souls. You are called in a special way. It pleases Me greatly though when others spend time immersed in My Passion, through structured prayer or silent contemplation. This will gain many graces for each soul in the world."* I must say in closing that this suffering was unpleasant and Jesus is wounded terribly by the indifference of man. We must all do more to console Him.

June 18, 2004
Blessed Mother

I am here, little one. Place your hands against your chest again and I will send great graces of peace and love to your little wounded heart. Jesus is so grateful to you. We must bring Him many souls today.

June 26, 2004
Jesus

I am with you. I am allowing you to see the enemy. In each of these events this morning, you have seen a glimpse of the forces pressing against what is good. Anne, it is for all of this that I use your suffering. I will continue to allow you to see the world through My eyes. I realize this is uncomfortable but if you remain united to Me, you will have every possible strength and consolation.

June 30, 2004

I don't know what to say about today's experience except that I was filled with a terrible feeling, which Jesus identified as the revulsion He feels when He is confronted by some sins. Today's was dreadful and even now I am having trouble shaking it off.

Jesus

What you feel is the revulsion I experience when priests who are arrogantly rebellious receive Me in the Eucharist. They are filled with sins of the flesh and delight in the paradox of presiding over the Great Sacrifice with blatant disrespect and insincerity. This is the ultimate in rebellion and I, Jesus Christ, experience this every day. You had great difficulty disengaging yourself, Anne, such is the dreadful filth of this experience. You said, "Lord, how on earth will I record this?" I dictate to you for that reason. Some things need not be recorded on earth but be assured, each act is recorded in heaven and recorded in My heart.

After a short period of the greatest difficulty, I am at peace.

July 2, 2004

Jesus was heavy-hearted today and said that chastisements would come with great loss of life. He asked me to kneel down and pray for these souls who would be taken abruptly. Jesus is not happy about this, but we must move through the storm in order to emerge on the other side.

July 9, 2004

Jesus is prepared and determined to begin this process of cleansing. He drew attention to the reference made to children who have never been exposed to goodness. He said there are many cases where even mothers school their children in evil ways from the time they are young. They do not apologize for, feel remorse about, or seek to amend their behavior in any way. These children have difficulty understanding goodness later and equate goodness with foolishness and stupidity. This is what they are taught. What struck me, and what Jesus was trying to convey to me, is the disregard the mother had for the fact that she was corrupting her child. This was a bad thing.

Jesus again made reference to the slaughter of abortions. He said when chastisements befall the earth, evil people who are choosing darkness move from ridiculing God and mocking Him to cursing Him. They say, in effect, "Look how cold and hateful God is to allow this to happen."

Jesus

In response I would like to say that at least I have given these souls a chance to live and an opportunity to make their decision to serve heaven or not to serve heaven, unlike current humanity, who slaughters the innocents before they are even fully formed. Who is the evil doer, I ask you? You will have these answers, Anne, because I am placing them in your heart. The slaughtered souls do not suffer in their eternity, in response to your unasked question. They are given opportunities to earn holiness here with Me. I am all justice. It is your world who suffers because these individuals had purposes. Your humanity rejected their brothers and sisters, refusing to make room for them in their selfishness. Woe to you, selfish ones. I am returning.

Please record the beautiful vision I gave to you.

Jesus showed me that in the darkness of the world there were shafts of light from people who were experiencing great infusions of grace from the messages. He has told me this and indicated this before but today I was aware of a woman kneeling in Eucharistic Adoration with her heart so joyful. He allowed me to experience the beautiful light of this soul that is seen by heaven, willing to serve, combined with the graces from this work. He said that He wants people to accept difficult days quietly and humbly.

July 12, 2004

Today Jesus brought me to Him and showed me a young boy, maybe eight or nine years old. The boy was in his room playing a video game on his bed. Jesus said that many parents are not home and if they are at home they are often unavailable to their children. Our Lord said that this boy was destined to be a great follower and do very big things for the Kingdom, but he was being given no formation. Because of this lack of formation, he would not be able to answer the call. He doesn't even know to listen for a call. Jesus said there are thousands like him. Jesus said that He wants this boy to be laying in his bed considering infinity and his possible role in infinity. He said that were the boy given the proper formation and knowledge and example, this child would grow to impact the world in a powerful way.

Jesus

As it is, Anne, he is being prepared to make money. This is a waste of My great gifts. Anne, his mother should be working quietly around the house, filling this child with the security he needs to be at peace and to consider his role in the universe. Alas, his mother is not at home. Someone who has little interest in him is caring for him and he knows it. His father now should quietly pass his room, and seeing his son daydreaming, should sit down with him and listen to his son's questions and intellectual stretches. His father is not at home to do this, though, because he is entertaining himself. Anne, My heart is so heavy at this waste of the Kingdom's greatest gifts. Your heart becomes heavy with Mine because you love Me and because you grieve for this boy's loneliness. You have asked how you can help this boy. I tell you that you can quickly complete the editing of Volume Six. Through it I will save many families, including this one. ANNE, I WANT MY FAMILIES BACK! (This was thundered at me.) *Please, get to work.*

Obviously, I went home and finished the editing that night. I must sound very virtuous. I assure my reader that Our Lord had told me earlier it was a priority but I felt like I was in a haze for about a week.

July 15, 2004

Our Lord showed me a gushing of black sludgy stuff flowing into some body of water. This makes Him angry and revolted. He said:

"When man began to destroy life in the womb, he also became disrespectful of life in other areas. My world was created for mankind and mankind should respect it. Do you see this desecration? The people responsible for this know that it is wrong according to man's law, but they also know it is wrong according to My law. They do not respect beauty, but seek power. Anne, I acquainted you with my revulsion at this destruction of My beautiful world. Yesterday I showed you how violent is the act of abortion. Do you understand how this hurts Me? Thank you for coming to Me. Thank you for making yourself available to be with Me in this unpleasantness. Thank you. You are having trouble coming out of it but that is also My will. It will leave you soon."

This has been dreadful. If there is ever a reader reading this they will say that I repeat myself. I guess our Lord is putting up with a lot lately. Honestly, the more time I spend in His heart, the more I wonder that He has been so patient. He is not pleased with this kind of ugly disobedience.

July 16, 2004
Jesus

Thank you for your suffering. You suffered more severely today because I am suffering severely today. Anne, some people are attempting to legitimize mortal sin through the marriage of two men and the marriage of two women. Anne, this is not My will. This is flagrant disobedience. Woe to those governments who sanction this desecration of the Sacrament of Matrimony. Anne, the weight of disobedience becomes too heavy for Me to carry. It must be released. You can barely manage this suffering. I feel the same. Your Jesus wearies. You may rest now.

Some thoughts from Anne on this entry: To be clear, Jesus suffers because he loves us and he wants the best for us. The topic of same-sex attraction can create suffering, confusion and disunity. Apostles, it is a distortion of Christianity to believe that sexual actions between people of the same gender are acceptable to God. These actions are outside of God's plan. It is also a distortion of Christianity to reject people, rather than actions we believe to be wrong. While it is important to discern our positions and refine our opinions, we must remember that the Lord's teaching is clear. God gives us the gift of sexuality with hope that we will all learn to exercise it morally. Imperfect humanity struggles, of course, and we know that "chastity includes an apprenticeship in self-mastery which is a training in human freedom" (CCC 2339).

We, followers of Christ, must avoid both morality without mercy and love without morality. Balance can always be found in the teachings of the Church and we must look for balance there.

July 23, 2004

Today Jesus spoke about His feelings of urgency in getting Volume Six out. He said that heaven is fighting to reclaim its families. He said that in these days, families are under attack as never before. He said each member, father, mother, and each child is targeted by the enemy in different ways. Families are wide open and vulnerable because in many homes there is no prayer.

If a family is following Christ at all, He sends many defenses and protections. This is why in Volume Six He spoke to mothers, fathers, and children. He said that if even one member of a family prays to Him, He can send graces by the thousands into the home. He appealed to children because often they are open to Him and have a form of genetic memory (my take on it), of purity and goodness and, of course, God. So if a child gets these messages and begins to pray, the door can be opened to heaven and Jesus can enter and literally save the entire family. I have been given a beautiful awareness of how critical Volume Six is to Him and to us.

Jesus then spoke about my early experiences. He explained that during that time He allowed a great deal of awareness and growth to occur to confirm me on my path. He said that once I was confirmed on the path, after I had received the call to join the Secular Franciscan Order (SFO) and accepted, He stopped the mystical experiences. He explained that all the growth then occurred below the surface, where I could not see or feel it. My obedience to Him in suffering and in my vocation was used to create a spiritual stamina that would support me later. Every so often when it was too heavy, the cross and perceived separation from Him, He would give me a beautiful experience of heaven or Him so I would know I was still on His path that He had chosen and prepared for me.

Jesus

My roots go far into your soul, My little slave. You have no idea how deeply I am entrenched in you. We did hard work during those years between then and now. You have never wavered in this mission. Anne, you have little understanding of how extraordinary is your service to Me. You are immovable in your commitment because of the depth of the roots that you allowed me to cultivate in your soul. Your commitment to Me is solid. Do not fear you will turn away. My cohort has been well prepared and My little group of apostles cooperates beautifully with Me. Truly, I am well pleased with your mission team. Now record our hillside conversation.

Today Jesus showed me a young woman. She was at an outdoor pool in a revealing bathing suit, which is the latest style wherever she is. She comes from a great deal of money and her hair, her nails, her legs, her clothes—everything—is pampered and seen to, as it were. I refer to waxing, dying, pedicures and manicures. Women will understand that not a spot on her body has been overlooked in an attempt to beautify.

Jesus is so discouraged and sad. He showed me a glimpse of what He had planned and intended for her. He was calling her to a vocation as a religious sister in an order of nursing to children. I saw her ministering to children of another race who were sick, but joyful.

Jesus said her formation has been ignored. Her mother left her when she, the girl, was quite young. Her father had a series of relationships with women, but none who cared greatly for this young woman. Jesus said her body and the bodies of many young women are being groomed by Satan to serve him. In other words, their bodies are seen as sexual tools for sexual pleasure and that is where this obsession with and emphasis on the beautifying of each and every area of the body comes from. Jesus said that not an area is overlooked in this process of preparing young girls for sin. Little emphasis is placed on cultivating their virtues and spiritual development, but rather on primping their bodies to be attractive. He asked why we would wonder that so many children are born outside of sacramental unions. We encourage this vacuous obsession with beautifying the body and then we are surprised when they use it to sin.

I asked Jesus about her mother and He said she is gone and has blocked out all graces, and He cannot work through her. I asked how this girl could be saved and He said she has an aunt who will read the messages, recognize her, and give them to her. Jesus' original plan will not be served, but she will turn to Him in great love and awareness and serve Him beautifully and fruitfully in another way. Jesus said the messages in Volume Six have a great deal of work to do and He said that the graces from Volume Six are unlimited in that everything asked for will be answered as far as families intervening for loved ones.

Brothers and sisters, if you viewed this young woman as I was allowed to, you would have been appalled, repulsed, and very aware of how seriously we are failing our youth. She is not a bad girl. She is a product of the upbringing we have allowed for her. This is a good girl who feels empty because in her soul she knows she is missing something.

I was deeply affected by this vision because at her age I would have been sunning myself, also, regretting that my father would not give me the money for the stylish bathing suit, the glamorous hair coloring, and the pedicure.

I want to convey to my brothers and sisters that the vision I saw of this beautiful young woman caring joyfully for the dark-skinned children was followed by the reality, which is that the babies are neglected and alone in their sickness and poverty. They are unloved. They are heaven's treasures, un-treasured. They suffer and die alone here, unwelcome on this dark planet that cares nothing for Jesus and His beautiful will. Truly, we need to get it together and get off this path. Condemn selfishness. I'm sorry, but this was dreadful. Very upsetting.

Jesus, to comfort me I think, also stated that as reprehensible as the devil's version of sexuality is, His view of sexuality is beautiful and grand. Jesus delights in the love and joy that take place between a married couple who love each other and care for each other. This view or attitude, heaven's view, was very beautiful and consoling and there was nothing uncomfortable or laughable about it. This made me happy to see and makes heaven happy.

July 30, 2004

Today Jesus showed me a man being beaten. It was dreadful. The man was imprisoned for a reason that was unclear. I asked our Lord if he was being beaten for his faith and Jesus said *"Yes,"* but that his captors had arrested him under the guise of a fabricated charge, not related to his religion. I hate this and I was a little upset, saying, "Jesus, how does this console you? How can this possibly be good or helpful?"

Jesus explained, *"It is not the violence that helps Me or consoles Me. You are feeling sickened, Anne, and filled with revulsion and grief. You feel these things because I feel these things upon witnessing this situation. Anne, look into this man's eyes. You see love. I am whispering the most sublime words of love directly to His soul. I am filling Him with an awareness of My Passion and his great unity to Me through his suffering. No. It is not the violence that I am consoled by, Anne. You of all people understand that. It is this servant's response to the violence that creates the most enormous waves of tenderness and mercy in My heart. These waves wash up on the shores of your world of darkness. Look. Look now at what is happening."*

Jesus indicates flares of light shooting out from the

layer of darkness that covers the earth. They rise to heaven. These are souls for whom this man's willing offering of suffering has obtained mercy and grace. They have repented and accepted God's mercy. This man's offering has saved souls. He is beautiful in his beaten state. I came out of it and Jesus said, *"Would you take back the suffering you have just experienced?"* Of course I answered, "No." I am grateful to keep Jesus company when His heart is heavy. He said, again, *"Look."* I saw additional shoots of light rising to heaven, first one, then three, then ten, then bursts of thirty or forty. Jesus said, *"This is what your suffering with Me has gained for the Kingdom. Now go in peace and never question the value of suffering."*

August 2, 2004

With the greatest of difficulty I presented myself for my time with Jesus this morning. He showed me the same man whom I had seen being beaten on Friday. Jesus said, *"Look closely. What do you see?"* I saw that this man's captors are Asian soldiers. The room is dirty. Our beautiful victim is on the floor. *"He is your Franciscan brother, My child. The resistance you felt when you were coming to Me today is the resistance he feels when he is being taken off to be beaten. Anne, you do not understand the value of your suffering and I am going to clarify it for you. You shouldered his resistance. Your brother in Francis walked to his torture with a heart overflowing with joy. Indeed, his joy is confounding his captors. His joy will eventually convert many in this joyless place. Anne, much of his joy is possible because of your suffering. You are shouldering much of his burden. You are truly his little Simon, lifting the foot of the cross. He knows there is a little soul in the world who suffers valiantly for him. You noted on Friday that his face was beautiful, his eyes calm and peaceful. I sit here on My hilltop and there is nothing obstructing our view between he and I. You have suffered all week. This man has basked in My warm loving gaze all week. Do you still doubt the value of your suffering? You are his little sister in Francis and I have paired you to help each other. Your heart is now light and joyful. My child, you are destined to be in this world but also in the heavenly world. We told you it would be difficult. This is an example of the difficulty. You will meet this man one day and you will know each other. Do not fear this work. You cannot imagine the graces flowing through it to your world."*

Well, Jesus has certainly turned me on my head. I will come willingly down to do this work in the future. I cannot describe the horrible resistance I felt in beginning this today. It's like a jeering and mocking crowd surrounded me. This man is beautiful and saintly and I have no objection to being paired with him and suffering for him. I thank Jesus and praise Him. I had the worst week of physical suffering and I must say that it gives me great pleasure to know that I was able to help this man, whom I love most tenderly. I asked Jesus, "Where is this man's brown robe, cord, etc…?"

Jesus replied, *"They have taken it from Him. They have stripped him of anything that relates to Me or to his vocation. It means nothing. They, like many evil ones, are trying to complete the impossible. They are trying to eradicate Christ in the souls of His followers."*

August 3, 2004

Today Jesus showed me something brief but compelling. He showed me a woman in her kitchen. Her home was beautiful. She was obviously wealthy. She was well-dressed with great style and she moved efficiently through her kitchen preparing a meal for her family. I'm having trouble recording this and Jesus is prompting me, saying, *"I showed you her face. What did you see?"*

Well, brothers and sisters, when He showed me her face, I was aware that she was very beautiful by the world's standards. But I could not see that, really, because I was looking with the eyes of our Savior. What I saw with His heavenly eyes was dreadful. I was fearful of meeting her gaze as I would not want to have those eyes fixed on me. She was horrible. The heavenly vision experienced her face as a mass of small serpents. She is dreadfully ugly, despite her well-kept physical beauty. Her eyes are cold and dead. It was very unpleasant and I took little glances and hurriedly looked away.

Jesus says, *"She is a servant to the enemy. Her countenance revolts you because there is a complete absence of goodness. She knows I am here. She meets My gaze with audacious hatred. This woman is active in her community, volunteering for charitable causes. She is considered a good mother and attends a Christian church service every week. Anne, I realize this was unpleasant and I thank you for your willingness to share My view. I show you this to compare this woman's face with the pure beauty of the dirt streaked and battered face of My beloved servant in captivity. Souls must learn to look with My eyes and they will not put such value on physical beauty. You should pray for this woman, of course. You do so each time you ask for the conversion of sinners."*

August 4, 2004

Today Jesus showed me a newborn baby girl. Her parents are holy followers who have prayed for a child for some time. This little girl is a gift to them and also to the world. She will be followed by two brothers. She will have a beautiful formation and her great spiritual gifts will be apparent from an early age. She will help our Lord in the times to come and will be very important in ushering in the Age of Obedience. I do not know when she was born but she is alive now.

Jesus

My child, you do not understand why I show you these things. You do not need to understand everything. This little servant's role will be confirmed by your prophecy. Be at peace. You are unwell and I seek today to clarify many things for you. I wish you to record for Me in your journal. That is all.

August 5, 2004

Jesus showed me the world from the hilltop. It moves along, turning. He said that during this time, because of the difficulty, He moves time faster or shortens the days so that we will move more quickly through these days. I was directed by a friend later to a reference in *Matthew* 24:22. *"And if those days had not been shortened, no one would be saved; but for the sake of the elect they will be shortened."* This is a mercy. Jesus said that during the darkness He will move time even more quickly and this is a great mercy indeed. Jesus talked about the great gifts that He gives souls and how He sends just the right things into the lives of young people and children so that the gifts He will want to use will be developed. He showed me how He had given me certain teachers and opportunities so that I would learn to write and speak with confidence. He said He was pleased when I began teaching because I remained consistent with what He wanted. It is a source of great satisfaction to God when this occurs.

He also showed me examples of souls who had been given great gifts but who used them to further their own agendas with regard to power or worldly acclaim. This almost always resulted from temptation for personal gain which the enemy uses to lure souls into his service. This displeases God because the gifts come from Him, not the enemy, and they should be used for God and God's desires, which always include helping others and furthering the Kingdom.

Jesus

Be assured, you will see Me act then. My graces will be withdrawn from the world and you will know that I have left the world to reap what they sow. Anne, this is a kindness. You do not want your children living in a world which is willing to accept debasement and exalt it as good. This world was not created to glorify evil, but to glorify good. I will not have this and this is the only merciful way to act. I am a God of mercy. A God of mercy moves to protect His children when they are threatened with eternal perdition. My holy souls will rest in My peace, even as their world changes. You must continue on your paths and leave everything to Me. Trust is your watchword, your constant. I will never abandon My own, but I will intervene in a rebellious world.

I want to say that Jesus is not overly angry, but very serious, and very firm. He showed me the network of holy souls and a great deal of holiness seems to originate from the Blessed Mother. Her touch seems to go on and on, connecting souls whom she converts. I do not walk away with the feeling that anything dreadful is happening. Not at all. I feel very confident in Him, and I have the strongest sense that we are in the best and safest of hands. I am so grateful, really, that our Lord sits on His hillside and watches this world and each of us in it. I urge everyone to glance His way and offer Him a beautiful smile of love. He is really so filled with goodness.

August 6, 2004

Today Jesus showed me a beautiful dark-skinned woman being dragged from a road back into the forest or brush by three soldiers. These were partisan type soldiers, not very officially fitted out but they had guns. They were dark-skinned and I suspect were fellow countrymen. She held a small child. The child was dropped at one point. The woman allowed the child to fall by the wayside in an effort to protect the baby girl from whatever was about to occur. The child simply sat, looking dazed and uncertain as the men dragged the mother away deeper into the woods. The mother stopped struggling and the three men systematically raped her.

I won't try to describe the ugliness of this scene. This woman has been raped before. She was raped some time ago by soldiers and the rape resulted in a pregnancy, which resulted in the baby girl who is sitting uncertainly waiting for her mother. The soldiers finish and leave her. She is not physically injured to a great degree, thank God, and is only concerned about her little one, whom she loves with a fierce tenderness. How she must worry about protecting this child because the child is destined to grow into a woman. The woman pulls herself together.

I would like to describe the scene, such is my rage, but I do not do so in the interest of protecting her dignity. The reason I would like to describe it is so that each and every man who behaves in this way will understand that Christ is watching and they will be held accountable. I hope they convert and find forgiveness, but I praise God for divine justice in these matters. This woman mercifully collects her child and cries. The child snuggles into her mother's neck and wraps her little arms around this poor woman. Our beautiful victim holds her baby and is consoled and steadied by her child. Jesus speaks.

Jesus

This woman is a favored servant of Mine. She is a Christian, converted as a result of the effort of a missionary. She thanks me all through the day for the sun, for the rain, for the beautiful things in nature that she credits to Me as the Creator. I love her most tenderly. Anne, she is a victim soul. You are angry and you are struggling with your anger at Me because you see that I watch this and you want Me to act upon these men. I will do so. Have no fear. As you say, they will reap what they sow. You know that the scene you witnessed is not unusual in your world. People are mistreated often in this way. You have labored hard to help others who suffer at the hands of evil men.

There are a few things I want to show you. First of all, look at the beauty of this child. One of the things that pierces your heart is the confused look on this little one's face. You also feel deeply the love of the mother for this child and see how the mother is comforted by the child. Even during the attack, which is not sexual on the part of the woman, merely physical, the mother's only concern is for her child, whom I have protected. This baby is the result of a previous rape. The act of rape is a desecration of a person. I want to tell you that the victim is an unwilling participant. A victim's beautiful sexuality, which is My gift to him or her, is not in any way involved in an act in which they have being coerced. An attack of this nature does not impact the beauty of a person's sexuality. That is theirs to give to another. Some try to take this from others but they cannot. A person who has been used in this way should never think that their beautiful sexuality is affected. It is not in any way affected. One cannot take sexuality from another. It must be given. It is a physical attack and with My help, a victim will heal.

You are angry at Me, Anne, because you are blaming Me for this. You were here with Me while this was occurring. I did not do this. I did not will this. I do not will this for any of My children. This is man being rebellious, following the guidance of My enemy, Satan. These men are answering "yes" to him. They are exulting in this evil act. Please do not be like My enemies in the world and blame Me for evil. This woman is My friend and I love her. She will spend eternity with Me. Her daughter will be instrumental in saving many souls, as will her mother. And yet, the daughter was the result of a rape. It is this I wish to speak about.

There are those on your earth, even some of My friends, who say that an abortion is acceptable if a mother has been raped and if the infant is the result of this wretched form of physical attack. Let me explain how this wounds Me.

The act of rape is a desecration of a person's body, as I have said. If I choose to act as the Creator at this time and send an infant, it is the greatest form of bringing good from evil, which I do often. I am actually very busy in this time bringing good from evil because I have so much evil to work with and less good. In defiance against this act of rape, I send an infant. Do you have any idea how special and precious are these little representatives of God as goodness? These are truly the greatest of gifts to your world. And yet many agree that because the earthly father of the infant was acting badly, it is justifiable to slaughter what I have created. Anne, if we slaughtered every infant whose father was behaving badly, we would have far fewer people in this world, even given the great number who are already rejected and slaughtered. This is the gravest, most distorted of logic. The father behaves badly so the child must be slaughtered. I reject this diabolical reasoning. So must you. It takes courage to speak the truth in your world, but I will send plenty of courage to any soul who takes up the cause of the unborn. These are truly My most favored servants.

Back to My precious little victim soul. She will live for her child. She will survive for her child and she has embraced this gift, seeing her daughter as the miracle of creation that she is. The greatest of joy will come from this little girl to her mother, whom she will treasure, and to your world. We will all reap the benefits of this mother's decision to allow this child to be born.

With regard to the evildoers, you have

been allowed to see how I view them. They are lost to Me at this moment. I also see them behaving like wild dogs. You will continue to pray for their conversion, as you do each time you pray for the conversion of sinners. They will be dealt with. I want you to understand something else.

There are those who read this who will be appalled at this act, and yet, they witness such acts on television and do not turn their televisions off. They provide a market for the enemy to glorify such acts of depravity by viewing them. Anytime you watch entertainment in which a woman's, man's, or child's body is being used for anything other than holy actions, you are culpable. I do not wish men to view women's bodies without proper attire unless they are united to them in matrimony. I do not wish men to have sexual relations unless they are united to a woman in matrimony. Sexuality comes from Me. It is My domain. The gross misuse of sexuality in this time offends Me greatly and brings down the greatest of evil and suffering to everyone. This cruel assault is an example. The widespread rebellion in sexual matters must cease.

August 9, 2004

Today Jesus showed me some beautiful things in this world. The visions were not extensive but I saw a forest, a perfect lake, streams, and all of this below His canvas of the sky. Jesus then showed me men taking down a vast area of trees in an irresponsible way. This was the only unpleasant part of the vision and it did not last long. He said that He is generally pleased with the efforts of those who seek to preserve nature. He is pleased that man is beginning to give consideration to this planet as a precious creation and seeking to preserve it. This is good. He said:

"This pleases me, Anne. There are those holy men and women who understand that the beauty of nature is to be respected and cherished. People should not haphazardly destroy the natural environment because through it I sustain humanity. This is disrespectful to Me as the Creator, and also disrespectful to those who are coming after. Yes, I am pleased by respect for the world I have created. I am not pleased when my children place nature above mankind. This is not My will. I created the world for man, not man for the world."

Jesus showed me a row of houses, modest in size but pretty.

"This is My will. I want homes for people. You notice that these are not overly big. Man does not require a great many rooms in His home. I did not create man to live like a king on earth, but in heaven. There are those to whom I give great financial blessings so that they can use their power and wealth to further My will. Few can withstand the temptation of this, however. At times I am forced to take wealth away from a person in order to save them. I have no qualms about this. It is better for a person to suffer on earth than to lose eternity. I do not want My children to live for an earthly home because they can begin to value it more than they value each other. This is not My will. My will always has to do with helping others. In summary, I am pleased with efforts to preserve this world but the motivations should be pure and holy."

August 10, 2004

Today I saw a woman on a beach with sand. I thought it was some kind of island but our Lord told me to look again. I was having trouble concentrating and did not really want to see this as I suspected it would not be good. Rather than an island, the backdrop behind the girl was a city. The earth began to rumble and I heard a roar. A large wave, a wall of water really, came in from the ocean and moved or rather crashed over the city. I did not see a big picture of this but had the awareness and saw small things, such as a car with people in it being hit like it was nothing. When I realized there were people in it I turned away. This was not nice, but I hardly need to say that. I did not have an easy time with this today and afterward feared that I had offended Jesus because I was again angry and thinking, 'What is the point of this?' When I finally came to my senses I felt badly and said to Jesus, "How do you feel?" He said He would record how He felt so we shall see now.

Jesus

I, also, feel the tragedy of what you witnessed, My poor friend. I know that you have difficulty with this, but you are My recorder and you must accurately record what you witness. Why has this happened

to this city and to these people? Sin, Anne, has brought this down upon these people.*
Anne, there are people behaving badly and there have always been people behaving badly, but in this time, more than in other times, good people are quiet. Few defend Me. You live in My world, which I created. I will not have a world where innocents are slaughtered.

*Please see footnote page 16.

August 11, 2004

I saw the same scene. The water on the shore began to recede fast and then the big wave came. Jesus said: *"I have sent many signs to mankind but they are ignored. This level of rebelliousness will not continue. For those who tell you that man is no worse than he ever was, let Me say this. Never in the history of humanity was the slaughter of so many met with so little resistance. The taking of an innocent life through abortion can never be My will. Do not view these scenes as punishment because I have no need to punish man in this way. I do have a need to get man's attention and when I allow man to reap what he has sown, calamities occur. Man then begins to consider his eternal soul and his entrance to eternity. Men, even those who are not following Me, consider what will happen when they meet Me. I want changes in this world and changes will occur. Be at peace because the good souls who lose their lives in these incidents are martyrs to the times. Souls following darkness who are taken will have an opportunity to repent. Consider your role in the coming of the Kingdom and trust that I will care for everything."*

August 12, 2004

Today I saw the same city again. Jesus said, *"Look. The waters are gone. What is different?"* Well, there were children with mothers, I saw flowers, and the ugly fence was gone. It's hard to say why exactly, but the last two days what I saw was a big dirty city. Today it seems more like a small town than a city. There is a man out on the street from a shop and he is talking to someone. You just don't see that in the city I saw yesterday. Yes, it could happen. But no, it usually does not. I heard church bells ringing. The woman with the small child stopped and prayed with her child. Jesus smiled at this.

He said, *"I show you this to give you hope and to make you understand how it should be and how it will be after the cleansing. People will be free to love Me and to move more slowly. Anne, the incident you saw was one of many. These upheavals in nature have been occurring and they have impacted many souls. But these are small things in comparison to the changes that are coming. People should not worry over why I am taking control. It is My affair. People should worry over following Me in their lives and completing the duties I have assigned to them."*

August 13, 2004

Today our Lord showed me the sky, but I was having great difficulty. I have been having difficulty and have become fearful. He said I am overly concerned about what people will think of these revelations. Anyway, after I settled down I saw the moon with the horrid dark red color. The world was dark, except for this red moon. Another terrible malevolent darkness began to spread over the world. It was not real, I do not think. I think I experienced it as darkness but it was a horrible presence gradually spreading over the earth. I knew it was the enemy of light. Jesus said: *"The enemy seeks out his final collaborators. When the moon turns to red, My child, the calamities will begin and there will be no break in the events. They will come one after the other. People who are prepared will feel the quietness in their souls. People who have rejected Me will either choose Me then, or take another step closer to hell. This time is near."*

I asked Jesus how He felt because I see it as my job to be concerned for Him. Lately I feel I am failing Him terribly. He is quiet, solemn. There is a heaviness about Him. He does not like this, clearly, but this is the way it's going to go. I did say, "Lord, you are all-powerful. This darkness is not in charge. Would You not just appear in the sky and say, 'Here I am. I am God. Change?' "

He replied, *"Anne, I have done that. I have appeared in many ways. My mother is appearing all over your world, begging her children to change. The world has Scripture, which many ignore. The world has prophecy, which many ridicule. The world has My presence in every holy soul. There are healers whom I have sent to inspire faith. You knew I was with you long before you experienced anything supernatural. How did you know? You knew because every soul knows that I am here. Some tell themselves I am not here in order to secure license, which they use to sin and draw others from Me. No, My child. It is not I who have failed. These words will save many. I am sending warnings from every corner of the world during this time. I am doing My part. Let every soul do theirs. We will save many, but we will lose many, and that is why My heart is heavy. Be at peace with this as you are doing your part to comfort Me by your obedience and your presence in My suffering."*

August 16, 2004

Today Jesus showed me the aftermath of the hurricane. I saw destruction, of course, trees down, power lines everywhere, and debris. He said, *"Look more closely. What do you see?"* I saw people cleaning up, but I saw people helping other people. Everywhere I looked I saw people assisting others with moving things and clearing things. I saw a woman who had the greatest peace in her face.

Jesus

"She is thinking of Me," Jesus said. *"Difficulties of this nature help people to understand that there is a force greater than man and that all they have built can be taken in a moment. This is a good lesson for mankind. I want people to help each other when difficult times come. But I also want people to learn from the experiences of others. If there is a group of people on your earth who are starving, all should be helping. When a storm comes that destroys property, all should be helping. You see this happening, Anne. Can you say this is a bad thing when it inspires people to serve each other and consider God? Often it is through the deepest darkness that we are able to find the light. Do you understand? I do not*

want My earthly children to suffer, and yet, as you know, suffering will come. Encourage souls not to waste these opportunities. You will leave these things behind when you come to heaven so you should not be overly attached to them while you are here. Souls practicing this detachment will not be distraught when they lose possessions and that is what I want for My children. I want detachment from the things of this world."

August 17, 2004

Today our Lord again talked about how some people would turn to Him in hardship, and how others would curse and blame Him. He has spoken of this before and it really is a no-win situation for Him. This is how the enemy works, though, in that when all is well, God is someone to be ridiculed and holy people are patronized. When all goes wrong, God is bad and people say the most terrible things about Him, as though they were following Him anyway. A woman phoned recently and was talking about the great difficulties she was having. Her son has autism but he is recovering beautifully and will very likely recover fully. She is understandably worn out as the recovery program is rigorous and relentless. But things are going really well for her in the prognosis. She said bitterly, "I'd like to know what kind of God He is, letting small children suffer like this." This was said with such anger and disdain that I felt like I had been slapped. I stammered and finally replied, "God is recovering your son for you. You should thank Him."

Jesus

You see, Anne, what I refer to when I say that they will hate Me regardless. This woman is tired and is worldly. She is comparing herself to others who have more and would seem to have an easier life. Her son is her great gift and through him this family receives many blessings. She does not see that. She lives for the world. Pray for her and do not fret for Me. I understand her fatigue. She will serve Me well later.

I want to draw attention to the comparison I made to those who live holy lives, detached in general from the world. If the general focus is on Me in a home, that home will not be as traumatized to lose worldly things.

You are watching the events in the world. You see people starving. You see many who have lost homes due to famine and war and events in nature. Do you understand, Anne, that souls are receiving these difficulties in different ways?

I compared your husband to another man. Your husband, if given those circumstances, would rise each day and serve his family in whatever circumstances he was given. He would not curse Me. He would not curse others. He would care for his family first and then use his abilities to serve others who were also struggling. This is how a holy man faces challenges. He would grieve, yes, but I could comfort him and his soul would reap splendid advantages from his difficulties. You have already seen that in your husband's case. His difficulties were part of his formation, as were your own.

Another man, living for the world and for his physical appetites, would curse Me. It is happening now and will increase as the troubles in your world increase. This other man, the one I use for an example, is not following Me. He does not sacrifice for Me and gives Me no credit at all for any good fortune that has come his way. He does the minimum amount of service to his family and spends his time entertaining himself and feeding his appetites and desires. When difficulties come his way, he will have to choose whether or not he will become a man of God or continue on his path to the enemy. The hardships that will come will force a choice on many souls. This is My will and this is why I am asking for such prayer from My followers. We must spread My words so that souls can begin to understand the times in which they live.

August 18, 2004

Jesus showed me the world from His hilltop. He directed my attention to the wave, which is a big event that will do great damage. He showed me in another area there were bombs being dropped because one country wanted to have power over another. In another area there was slaughter and the word genocide came to my mind. There were terrible events in nature. There was disease, and killing all over. Jesus said, *"Do you understand now what I mean when I say upheaval?"* Well, I don't know whether I did or not, but I do now. The world is going to be in serious upheaval.

Jesus

Thank you. I know this is unpleasant but I also know that you are willing through your acts of obedience to Me. Do not worry that you sometimes serve in fear or sometimes in sadness. You serve. That is what I will consider when I give you the reward you have earned so beautifully. You have a great deal of service ahead of you.

Now, we have clarified what I mean when I use the word upheaval. The events you witnessed, which are representative of the many events that will occur, will begin soon. They will come quickly, one after the

*other and you will know that I have
spoken of this as the time of upheaval.*

*In response to your question of whether or
not I want to clarify when soon is, My
answer to you was "no." I will not clarify
soon to you, little servant, because you are
heavily burdened as it is and do not need
that additional weight.* (I thanked Him very
sincerely.) *You are welcome.*

*Can you see why I want My words
distributed? I want to be with souls and I
want souls to know that I am with them.
They will face these events in peace if they
have practiced relying on Me and trusting
Me. They will face death differently.*

*Some will die during this time. We all face
death if we are human and that is what I
want you to stress to people when you
speak. Refer to the message I gave to you
when you asked to read the messages of
another. This was very human of you,
Anne, so do not be ashamed. You wanted to
know what would happen. I told you that
you would live for a time and then you
would die. It was not My will that you
knew more than that from someone other
than Me, your Jesus. I do not like souls
seeking information to frighten others.
Warn others, yes. But you see that even*

when I am giving news that could frighten, I am gentle and loving and concentrate on the Truth, which is that heaven will be actively involved in the events on earth and in the lives of those who welcome us. I tell you again, do not be afraid. There is no need.

I just want to say that I am often afraid and I know Jesus is with me and I know Jesus will not leave me. But I am often afraid in my humanity. So if a reader is afraid, I think that reader should not feel he or she is lacking. It is a good area for us to work on in contemplative prayer. Jesus would not keep telling us this if He did not think it was a problem for us to trust Him. He understands. Also, knowing Jesus, there really is no reason to fear. He never lies, of course, and He will never leave us alone. I need to practice trusting more so if you are sometimes afraid, you are like me.

August 19, 2004
Jesus

I have many reasons for allowing souls to glimpse the future. I am seeking a great detachment during these times. My words and the graces attached to them will help souls with this process. I am Jesus Christ and I am seeking out My children. I want to protect you. All who know Me, know that I am gentle, indeed the most gentle of men. My Divinity is also gentle and I desire that souls be at peace. It is for this reason I am so generous with My words and graces. I am sending everything your world needs to move through difficult times with confidence and joy. You must do your part, little children.

You must heed My words and you must spread them. The merit gained in the spread of these words will astound you because I am asking this of you and souls who do this work are saying "yes" to Me. I am grateful more than you realize, faithful ones. Now be brave and assist your brothers and sisters by giving them these words. You will be well rewarded in heaven. Peace. When you do not have peace in your heart, stop what you are doing and pray. I will restore peace to your soul and you will then be happier and more effective. Remember that I am Jesus and I am God. I will see to everything.

September 21, 2004
Jesus

My little souls see clearly how I am working in the world. I am putting my servants together in groups to serve Me most effectively. Be confident in My guidance in your lives. I will not let you falter, nor will I give you a mission and then fail to direct its course. There is nothing that should frighten My apostles. You are My friends, dear ones. You are entitled to every heavenly consideration. You must petition heaven for anything you need to accomplish your work and you will have it.

Do not fear the cross. Remember that salvation for many often comes through one person's agreement to carry a little cross. Do not separate the two issues and you will be joyful. Your cross can equal your brother's salvation. This was My thought in everything. While carrying the cross, I thought of you. When you carry a cross, think of Me. Together We will proceed.

Appendix

The Lay Apostolate of Jesus Christ the Returning King

We seek to be united to Jesus in our daily work, and through our vocations, in order to obtain graces for the conversion of sinners. Through our cooperation with the Holy Spirit, we will allow Jesus to flow through us to the world, bringing His light. We do this in union with Mary, our Blessed Mother, with the Communion of Saints, with all of God's holy angels, and with our fellow lay apostles in the world.

Guidelines for Lay Apostles

As lay apostles of Jesus Christ the Returning King, we agree to perform our basic obligations as practicing Catholics. Additionally, we will adopt the following spiritual practices, as best we can:

1. **Allegiance Prayer** and **Morning Offering**, plus a brief prayer for the Holy Father
2. **Eucharistic Adoration**, one hour per week
3. **Prayer Group Participation**, monthly, at which we pray the Luminous Mysteries of the Holy Rosary and read the Monthly Message
4. **Monthly Confession**
5. Further, we will follow the example of Jesus Christ as set out in the Holy Scripture, treating all others with His patience and kindness.

Allegiance Prayer

Dear God in Heaven, I pledge my allegiance to You. I give You my life, my work and my heart. In turn, give me the grace of obeying Your every direction to the fullest possible extent. Amen.

Morning Offering

O Jesus, through the Immaculate Heart of Mary, I offer You the prayers, works, joys and sufferings of this day, for all the intentions of Your Sacred Heart, in union with the Holy Sacrifice of the Mass throughout the world, in reparation for my sins, and for the intentions of the Holy Father. Amen.

Prayer for the Holy Father

Blessed Mary, Mother of Jesus, protect our Holy Father, Benedict XVI, and bless his intentions.

Five Luminous Mysteries

1. The Baptism of Jesus
2. The Wedding at Cana
3. The Proclamation of the Kingdom of God
4. The Transfiguration
5. The Institution of the Eucharist

Promise from Jesus to His Lay Apostles

May 12, 2005

Your message to souls remains constant. Welcome each soul to the rescue mission. You may assure each lay apostle that just as they concern themselves with My interests, I will concern Myself with theirs. They will be placed in My Sacred Heart and I will defend and protect them. I will also pursue complete conversion of each of their loved ones. So you see, the souls who serve in this rescue mission as My beloved lay apostles will know peace. The world cannot make this promise as only Heaven can bestow peace on a soul. This is truly Heaven's mission and I call every one of Heaven's children to assist Me. You will be well rewarded, My dear ones.

Prayers taken from The Volumes

Prayers to God the Father

"What can I do for my Father in Heaven?"

"I trust You, God. I offer You my pain in the spirit of acceptance and I will serve You in every circumstance."

"God my Father in Heaven, You are all mercy. You love me and see my every sin. God, I call on You now as the Merciful Father. Forgive my every sin. Wash away the stains on my soul so that I may once again rest in complete innocence. I trust You, Father in Heaven. I rely on You. I thank You. Amen."

"God my Father, calm my spirit and direct my path."

"God, I have made mistakes. I am sorry. I am Your child, though, and seek to be united to You."

"I believe in God. I believe Jesus is calling me. I believe my Blessed Mother has requested my help. Therefore I am going to pray on this day and every day."

"God my Father, help me to understand."

Prayers to Jesus

"Jesus, I give You my day."

"Jesus, how do You want to use me on this day? You have a willing servant in me, Jesus. Allow me to work for the Kingdom."

"Lord, what can I do today to prepare for Your coming? Direct me, Lord, and I will see to Your wishes."

"Lord, help me."

"Jesus, love me."

Prayers to the Angels

"Angels from Heaven, direct my path."

"Dearest angel guardian, I desire to serve Jesus by remaining at peace. Please obtain for me the graces necessary to maintain His divine peace in my heart."

Prayers for a Struggling Soul

"Jesus, what do You think of all this? Jesus, what do You want me to do for this soul? Jesus, show me how to bring You into this situation."

"Angel guardian, thank you for your constant vigil over this soul. Saints in Heaven, please assist this dear angel."

Prayers for Children

"God in Heaven, You are the Creator of all things. Please send Your graces down upon our world."

"Jesus, I love You."

"Jesus, I trust in You. Jesus, I trust in You. Jesus, I trust in You."

"Jesus, I offer You my day."

"Mother Mary, help me to be good."

How to Recite the Chaplet of Divine Mercy

The Chaplet of Mercy is recited using ordinary Rosary beads of five decades. The Chaplet is preceded by two opening prayers from the *Diary* of Saint Faustina and followed by a closing prayer.

1. Make the Sign of the Cross

In the name of the Father, and of the Son, and of the Holy Spirit. Amen.

2. Optional Opening Prayers

You expired, Jesus, but the source of life gushed forth for souls, and the ocean of mercy opened up for the whole world. O Fount of Life, unfathomable Divine Mercy, envelop the whole world and empty Yourself out upon us.

O Blood and Water, which gushed forth from the Heart of Jesus as a fountain of mercy for us, I trust in You!

3. Our Father

Our Father, who art in Heaven, hallowed be Thy name. Thy Kingdom come. Thy will be done on earth as it is in Heaven. Give us this day our daily bread. And forgive us our trespasses, as we forgive those who trespass against us. And lead us not into temptation, but deliver us from evil. Amen.

4. Hail Mary

Hail Mary, full of grace, the Lord is with thee. Blessed art thou among women, and blessed is the fruit of thy womb, Jesus. Holy Mary, Mother of God, pray for us sinners, now and at the hour of our death. Amen.

5. The Apostles' Creed

I believe in God, the Father Almighty, Creator of Heaven and earth. I believe in Jesus Christ, His only Son, our Lord. He was conceived by the power of the Holy Spirit and born of the Virgin Mary. He suffered under Pontius Pilate, was crucified, died, and was buried. He descended to the dead. On the third day He rose again. He ascended into Heaven, and is seated at the right hand of the Father. He will come again to judge the living and the dead. I believe in the Holy Spirit, the holy Catholic Church, the Communion of Saints, the forgiveness of sins, the resurrection of the body, and life everlasting. Amen.

6. The Eternal Father

Eternal Father, I offer You the Body and Blood, Soul and Divinity of Your dearly beloved Son, our Lord, Jesus Christ, in atonement for our sins and those of the whole world.

7. On the Ten Small Beads of Each Decade

For the sake of His Sorrowful Passion, have mercy on us and on the whole world.

8. Repeat for the remaining decades

Saying the "Eternal Father" (6) on the "Our Father" bead and then 10 "For the sake of His Sorrowful Passion" (7) on the following "Hail Mary" beads.

9. Conclude with Holy God

Holy God, Holy Mighty One, Holy Immortal One, have mercy on us and on the whole world.

10. Optional Closing Prayer

Eternal God, in whom mercy is endless and the treasury of compassion inexhaustible, look kindly upon us and increase Your mercy in us, that in difficult moments we might not despair nor become despondent, but with great confidence submit ourselves to Your holy will, which is Love and Mercy itself.

To learn more about the image of The Divine Mercy, the Chaplet of Divine Mercy and the series of revelations given to St. Faustina Kowalska please contact:

Marians of the Immaculate Conception
Stockbridge, Massachusetts 01263
Telephone 800-462-7426
www.marian.org

How to Pray the Rosary

1. Make the Sign of the Cross and say the "Apostles Creed."
2. Say the "Our Father."
3. Say three "Hail Marys."
4. Say the "Glory be to the Father."
5. Announce the First Mystery; then say the "Our Father."
6. Say ten "Hail Marys," while meditating on the Mystery.
7. Say the "Glory be to the Father." After each decade say the following prayer requested by the Blessed Virgin Mary at Fatima: "O my Jesus, forgive us our sins, save us from the fires of hell, lead all souls to Heaven, especially those in most need of Thy mercy."
8. Announce the Second Mystery: then say the "Our Father." Repeat 6 and 7 and continue with the Third, Fourth, and Fifth Mysteries in the same manner.
9. Say the "Hail, Holy Queen" on the medal after the five decades are completed.

As a general rule, depending on the season, the Joyful Mysteries are said on Monday and Saturday; the Sorrowful Mysteries on Tuesday and Friday;

the Glorious Mysteries on Wednesday and Sunday; and the Luminous Mysteries on Thursday.

Papal Reflections of the Mysteries

The Joyful Mysteries

The Joyful Mysteries are marked by the joy radiating from the event of the Incarnation. This is clear from the very first mystery, the Annunciation, where Gabriel's greeting to the Virgin of Nazareth is linked to an invitation to messianic joy: "Rejoice, Mary." The whole of salvation... had led up to this greeting. (Prayed on Mondays and Saturdays, and optional on Sundays during Advent and the Christmas Season.)

The Luminous Mysteries

Moving on from the infancy and the hidden life in Nazareth to the public life of Jesus, our contemplation brings us to those mysteries which may be called in a special way "Mysteries of Light." Certainly, the whole mystery of Christ is a mystery of light. He is the "Light of the world" (John 8:12). Yet this truth emerges in a special way during the years of His public life. (Prayed on Thursdays.)

The Sorrowful Mysteries

The Gospels give great prominence to the Sorrowful Mysteries of Christ. From the beginning, Christian piety, especially during the Lenten devotion of the Way of the Cross, has focused on the individual moments of the Passion, realizing that here is found the culmination of the revelation of God's love and the source of our salvation. (Prayed on Tuesdays and Fridays, and optional on Sundays during Lent.)

The Glorious Mysteries

"The contemplation of Christ's face cannot stop at the image of the Crucified One. He is the Risen One!" The Rosary has always expressed this knowledge born of faith and invited the believer to pass beyond the darkness of the Passion in order to gaze upon Christ's glory in the Resurrection and Ascension... Mary herself would be raised to that same glory in the Assumption. (Prayed on Wednesdays and Sundays.)

From the *Apostolic Letter The Rosary of the Virgin Mary*, Pope John Paul II, Oct. 16, 2002.

Prayers of the Rosary

The Sign of the Cross

In the name of the Father, and of the Son, and of the Holy Spirit. Amen.

The Apostles' Creed

I believe in God, the Father Almighty, Creator of Heaven and earth. I believe in Jesus Christ, His only Son, our Lord. He was conceived by the power of the Holy Spirit and born of the Virgin Mary. He suffered under Pontius Pilate, was crucified, died, and was buried. He descended to the dead. On the third day He rose again. He ascended into Heaven, and is seated at the right hand of the Father. He will come again to judge the living and the dead. I believe in the Holy Spirit, the holy Catholic Church, the Communion of Saints, the forgiveness of sins, the resurrection of the body, and life everlasting. Amen.

Our Father

Our Father, who art in Heaven, hallowed be Thy name. Thy Kingdom come. Thy will be done on earth as it is in Heaven. Give us this day our daily bread. And forgive us our trespasses, as we forgive those who trespass against us. And lead us not into temptation, but deliver us from evil. Amen.

Hail Mary

Hail Mary, full of grace, the Lord is with thee. Blessed art thou among women, and blessed is the fruit of thy womb, Jesus. Holy Mary, Mother of God, pray for us sinners, now and at the hour of our death. Amen.

Glory Be to the Father

Glory be to the Father, and to the Son, and to the Holy Spirit. As it was in the beginning, is now, and ever shall be, world without end. Amen.

Hail Holy Queen

Hail, Holy Queen, Mother of Mercy, our life, our sweetness and our hope. To thee do we cry, poor banished children of Eve. To thee do we send up our sighs, mourning and weeping in this valley of tears. Turn then, most gracious Advocate, thine eyes of mercy towards us. And after this, our exile, show unto us the blessed fruit of thy womb, Jesus. O clement, O loving, O sweet Virgin Mary!

Pray for us, O Holy Mother of God.
That we may be made worthy of the promises of Christ.

The Mysteries

First Joyful Mystery:
The Annunciation

And when the angel had come to her, he said, "Hail, full of grace, the Lord is with thee. Blessed art thou among women." *(Luke* 1:28)

> One *Our Father*, Ten *Hail Marys*,
> One *Glory Be*, etc.

Fruit of the Mystery: ***Humility***

Second Joyful Mystery:
The Visitation

Elizabeth was filled with the Holy Spirit and cried out in a loud voice: "Blest are you among women and blest is the fruit of your womb."*(Luke* 1:41-42)

> One *Our Father*, Ten *Hail Marys*,
> One *Glory Be*, etc.

Fruit of the Mystery: ***Love of Neighbor***

Third Joyful Mystery:
The Birth of Jesus

She gave birth to her first-born Son and wrapped Him in swaddling clothes and laid Him in a manger, because there was no room for them in the place where travelers lodged. *(Luke* 2:7)

> One *Our Father*, Ten *Hail Marys*,
> One *Glory Be*, etc.

Fruit of the Mystery: ***Poverty***

Fourth Joyful Mystery:
The Presentation

When the day came to purify them according to the law of Moses, the couple brought Him up to Jerusalem so that He could be presented to the Lord, for it is written in the law of the Lord, "Every first-born male shall be consecrated to the Lord."

(Luke 2:22-23)

One Our Father, Ten Hail Marys,
One Glory Be, etc.

Fruit of the Mystery: ***Obedience***

Fifth Joyful Mystery:
The Finding of the Child Jesus in the Temple

On the third day they came upon Him in the temple sitting in the midst of the teachers, listening to them and asking them questions.   (Luke 2:46)

One Our Father, Ten Hail Marys,
One Glory Be, etc.

Fruit of the Mystery: ***Joy in Finding Jesus***

First Luminous Mystery:
The Baptism of Jesus

And when Jesus was baptized… the heavens were opened and He saw the Spirit of God descending like a dove, and alighting on Him, and lo, a voice from heaven, saying "this is My beloved Son," with whom I am well pleased."   (Matthew 3:16-17)

One Our Father, Ten Hail Marys,
One Glory Be, etc.

Fruit of the Mystery: ***Openness to the Holy Spirit***

Second Luminous Mystery:
The Wedding at Cana

His mother said to the servants, "Do whatever He tells you."… Jesus said to them, "Fill the jars with water." And they filled them up to the brim.

(John 2:5-7)

One *Our Father*, Ten *Hail Marys*,
One *Glory Be*, etc.

Fruit of the Mystery: ***To Jesus through Mary***

Third Luminous Mystery:
The Proclamation of the Kingdom of God

"And preach as you go, saying, 'The kingdom of heaven is at hand.' Heal the sick, raise the dead, cleanse lepers, cast out demons. You received without pay, give without pay." *(Matthew* 10:7-8)

One *Our Father*, Ten *Hail Marys*,
One *Glory Be*, etc.

Fruit of the Mystery: ***Repentance and Trust in God***

Fourth Luminous Mystery:
The Transfiguration

And as He was praying, the appearance of His countenance was altered and His raiment become dazzling white. And a voice came out of the cloud saying, "This is My Son, My chosen; listen to Him!

(Luke 9:29, 35)

One *Our Father*, Ten *Hail Marys*,
One *Glory Be*, etc.

Fruit of the Mystery: ***Desire for Holiness***

Fifth Luminous Mystery:
The Institution of the Eucharist

And He took bread, and when He had given thanks He broke it and gave it to them, saying, "This is My body which is given for you."… And likewise the cup after supper, saying, "This cup which is poured out for you is the new covenant in My blood."

(*Luke* 22:19-20)

One *Our Father*, Ten *Hail Marys*,
One *Glory Be*, etc.

Fruit of the Mystery: ***Adoration***

First Sorrowful Mystery:
The Agony in the Garden

In His anguish He prayed with all the greater intensity, and His sweat became like drops of blood falling to the ground. Then He rose from prayer and came to His disciples, only to find them asleep, exhausted with grief. (*Luke* 22:44-45)

One *Our Father*, Ten *Hail Marys*,
One *Glory Be*, etc.

Fruit of the Mystery: ***Sorrow for Sin***

Second Sorrowful Mystery:
The Scourging at the Pillar

Pilate's next move was to take Jesus and have Him scourged. (*John* 19:1)

One *Our Father*, Ten *Hail Marys*,
One *Glory Be*, etc.

Fruit of the Mystery: ***Purity***

Third Sorrowful Mystery:
The Crowning with Thorns

They stripped off His clothes and wrapped Him in a scarlet military cloak. Weaving a crown out of thorns they fixed it on His head, and stuck a reed in His right hand… *(Matthew* 27:28-29)

One *Our Father*, Ten *Hail Marys*,
One *Glory Be*, etc.

Fruit of the Mystery: ***Courage***

Fourth Sorrowful Mystery:
The Carrying of the Cross

… carrying the cross by Himself, He went out to what is called the Place of the Skull (in Hebrew, Golgotha). *(John* 19:17)

One *Our Father*, Ten *Hail Marys*,
One *Glory Be*, etc.

Fruit of the Mystery: ***Patience***

Fifth Sorrowful Mystery:
The Crucifixion

Jesus uttered a loud cry and said, "Father, into Your hands I commend My spirit." After He said this, He expired. *(Luke* 23:46)

One *Our Father*, Ten *Hail Marys*,
One *Glory Be*, etc.

Fruit of the Mystery: ***Perseverance***

First Glorious Mystery:
The Resurrection

You need not be amazed! You are looking for Jesus of Nazareth, the one who was crucified. He has been raised up; He is not here. See the place where they laid Him." *(Mark* 16:6)

One *Our Father*, Ten *Hail Marys*,
One *Glory Be*, etc.

Fruit of the Mystery: ***Faith***

Second Glorious Mystery:
The Ascension

Then, after speaking to them, the Lord Jesus was taken up into Heaven and took His seat at God's right hand. *(Mark* 16:19)

One *Our Father*, Ten *Hail Marys*,
One *Glory Be*, etc.

Fruit of the Mystery: ***Hope***

Third Glorious Mystery:
The Descent of the Holy Spirit

All were filled with the Holy Spirit. They began to express themselves in foreign tongues and make bold proclamation as the Spirit prompted them.

(Acts 2:4)

One *Our Father*, Ten *Hail Marys*,
One *Glory Be*, etc.

Fruit of the Mystery: ***Love of God***

Fourth Glorious Mystery:
The Assumption

You are the glory of Jerusalem... you are the splendid boast of our people... God is pleased with what you have wrought. May you be blessed by the Lord Almighty forever and ever.

(Judith 15:9-10)

One *Our Father*, Ten *Hail Marys*,
One *Glory Be*, etc.

Fruit of the Mystery: ***Grace of a Happy Death***

Fifth Glorious Mystery:
The Coronation

A great sign appeared in the sky, a woman clothed with the sun, with the moon under her feet, and on her head a crown of twelve stars. *(Revelation* 12:1)

One *Our Father*, Ten *Hail Marys*,
One *Glory Be*, etc.

Fruit of the Mystery: ***Trust in Mary's Intercession***

This book is part of a non-profit mission. Our Lord has requested that we spread these words internationally. Please help us.

In Ireland:
Direction For Our Times
The Hague Building
Cullies
Cavan
County Cavan

+353-(0)49-437-3040
contactus@dfot.ie

Registered Charity CHY17298

In the USA:
Direction For Our Times
9000 West 81st Street
Justice, Illinois 60458

708-496-9300
contactus@directionfor
ourtimes.org

A 501(c)(3) Organization

Monthly Messages

For seven years Jesus gave Anne a message for the world on the first day of every month. Each month the apostolate reads one of these monthly messages. To receive the monthly messages you may access our website at **www.directionforourtimes.org** or call us at one of our offices to be placed on our mailing list.

We have also printed a book which contains all of the monthly messages. It can be purchased through our website as well.

The Volumes

Direction for Our Times
as given to Anne, a lay apostle

The Volumes are now available in PDF format for
free download and printing from our website:
www.directionforourtimes.org.
We encourage everyone to print and distribute them.

The Volumes are also available at your local bookstore.

The "Heaven Speaks" Booklets

Direction for Our Times
as given to Anne, a lay apostle

The following booklets are available individually from Direction for Our Times:

Heaven Speaks About Abortion
Heaven Speaks About Addictions
Heaven Speaks to Victims of Clerical Abuse
Heaven Speaks to Consecrated Souls
Heaven Speaks About Depression
Heaven Speaks About Divorce
Heaven Speaks to Prisoners
Heaven Speaks to Soldiers
Heaven Speaks About Stress
Heaven Speaks to Young Adults

Heaven Speaks to Those Away from the Church
Heaven Speaks to Those Considering Suicide
Heaven Speaks to Those Who Do Not Know Jesus
Heaven Speaks to Those Who Are Dying
Heaven Speaks to Those Who Experience Tragedy
Heaven Speaks to Those Who Fear Purgatory
Heaven Speaks to Those Who Have Rejected God
Heaven Speaks to Those Who Struggle to Forgive
***Heaven Speaks to Those Who Suffer from
    Financial Need***
***Heaven Speaks to Parents Who Worry About
    Their Children's Salvation***

All twenty of the "Heaven Speaks" booklets are now available in PDF format for free download and printing from our website www.directionforourtimes.org. We encourage everyone to print and distribute these booklets.

Other books by Anne, a lay apostle

Climbing the Mountain
Discovering your path to holiness
Anne's experiences of Heaven

The Mist of Mercy
Spiritual Warfare
Anne's experiences of Purgatory

Serving In Clarity
A Guide for Lay Apostles
of Jesus Christ the Returning King

In Defense of Obedience
and
Reflections on the Priesthood
Two Essays on topics close to the Heart of Jesus

Lessons in Love
Moving Toward Divine Intimacy

Whispers from the Cross
Reclaiming the Church
Through Personal Holiness